Storymaking and Creative Groupwork with Older People

of related interest

Hearing the Voice of People with Dementia
Opportunities and Obstacles
Malcolm Goldsmith
ISBN 1 85302 406 6

Not Too Late
Psychotherapy and Ageing
Ann Orbach
ISBN 1 85302 380 9

Reflections on Therapeutic Storymaking
The Use of Stories in Groups
Alida Gersie
ISBN 1 85302 272 1

Discovering the Self through Drama and Movement
The Sesame Approach
Edited by Jenny Pearson
ISBN 1 85302 384 1

Quality of Life
Philip Seed and Greg Lloyd
ISBN 1 85302 413 9

Storymaking and Creative Groupwork with Older People

Paula Crimmens

Jessica Kingsley Publishers
London and Bristol, Pennsylvania

First published in the United Kingdom in 1998 by
Jessica Kingsley Publishers Ltd
116 Pentonville Road
London N1 9JB, England
and
1900 Frost Road, Suite 101
Bristol, PA 19007, U S A

Copyright © 1998

Library of Congress Cataloging in Publication Data
A CIP catalogue record for this book is available from the Library of Congress

British Library Cataloguing in Publication Data
A CIP catalogue record for this book is available from the British Library

ISBN 1 85302 440 6

Printed and Bound in Great Britain by
Athenaeum Press, Gateshead, Tyne and Wear

This book is dedicated to Alison Kelly, my friend and colleague, from whom I learned so much and without whom this book would not have been possible.

Acknowledgements

I would like to acknowledge all the people who assisted me in running the groups that have provided so much of the material for this book, as well as all the group members. They include Barry White at St Pancras, Maggie Elwes at Turtle Key and Sheila Smith at Athlone House. I have tremendous gratitude for the ongoing support of Margaret Butterworth of CRAC Dementia and Carole Evans of Carers of the Elderly. Also, many thanks to Jane Jason of The Joseph Levy Charitable Foundation. Thanks go to my supervisor, Rex Bradley, at Spectrum and Sue Askew for reading parts of the book and giving me feedback. Thanks to Charles Catton at Jessica Kingsley for his patience. And last, but not least, thank you to my husband, Tom Cooper, for his support and encouragement.

Contents

ACKNOWLEDGEMENTS

INTRODUCTION   9

1 Why Groups?   14

Aims in organising a group   15
Contact and connection   16
The group as opportunity for sharing and community   21
Enjoyment   22
Self-esteem   22
Reducing boredom and increasing interest   23
Maintaining and extending people's physical and mental abilities 23
Activities as an opportunity to use the person-centred approach 25

2 The Story Session   30

Assistance in running the group   32
The make-up of a group   33
The format of a session   33

3 Stories that Contain a Central Elderly Figure   51

Yaaba   53
Babka and the Golden Bird   57
Granny Evergreen   62
The Old Woman and the Tree Children   63
The Three Blue Hats   67
The Pedlar of Swaffham   72
The Three Dancing Princesses   78

4 The Theme of Loss in the Lives of Elderly People   83

Demeter and Persephone   93
Coyote and Eagle   100
The Crescent Moon Bear   103

5 Loss of Home and Possessions 108

The Water of Life 109
Maple Leaf Devil 114
The Bird of Happiness 118
The Widow and the Honey Pots 123
The Shining Fish 126
How the Villagers found Wisdom 129

6 The Theme of Marriage and the Joy of Union 134

Savitri and Satyavan 140
Gawain and Lady Ragnell 146
The Blue Flower of Beechy Hill 150
The Black Bull of Norway 153
Tam Lin 158
The Frog Princess 163
The Boa and the Mango Tree 168

EPILOGUE 173

Introduction

This book is intended to be a resource book for professionals working with older men and women. As the title suggests, its main concern is groupwork but it also gives information on working creatively one to one.

This book is for everyone who loves stories. It is a self-help book with ideas and suggestions on how to use the stories and adapt them to suit the nature of the audience. It gives information and guidelines on how to facilitate a group's enjoyment and participation in a story session with the use of objects.

The book has grown out of my own experience as both a drama therapist working with elderly people themselves and more latterly as a trainer working with staff who work in this field.

It comes from my very deeply held belief in the importance of working with older people, work that in the past has been as undervalued and marginalised as elderly people themselves. Times, however, are changing. Demographics tell us that soon there will be as many over the age of retirement as under. Hardly a week goes by without some aspect of old age receiving attention in the media and elderly people themselves, both here and in the US, are becoming more politicised on their own behalf. There is a movement emerging that aims to balance the prevalent, cultural stereotype of older people as being burdensome and a drain on resources, with a picture that includes wisdom, experience, respect and dignity.

So what does becoming an elder mean? It means reaching maturity, developing wisdom, having an overview, having more time. What is the role of the elder? This book gives ideas and images for the role drawn from contemporary life and the lives of other cultures in the form of stories.

Old age becomes a stage in a process that begins with birth and reaches its maturity in later years, rather than a thing to be dreaded and avoided. It is a time of reflecting upon the joys and sadnesses of a life lived.

A lot of the elderly people I work with now have lived through two world wars. They've worked, played, raised families, made their choices for better or worse. They've been headmasters, factory girls, captains in the navy, models, carpenters and debutantes. They arrive at the end of their lives and there's a wasteland where there used to be a home and a job, spouse or family; there's an institution that's been paid to look after them and sometimes little acknowledgement of all that history and who they are. In the work that I do I seek to redress that balance.

I began working with elderly people in 1988 after training as a Sesame movement and drama therapist at The Central School of Speech and Drama, London. My first piece of work was with a group in Athlone House in Hampstead. Here most people were in wheelchairs and very frail. A lot had suffered strokes and had use of only one side of the body. Some had speech and hearing impairments. The energy in the group was very low. For most people, Athlone would be their final home. Some people had their own rooms, which although small afforded a measure of privacy and a bit more space for one's things. Others lived on a ward where one's own space comprised a bed and a locker.

Those first sessions were very difficult. I worked with another drama therapist, who proved invaluable. Such a lot of our training had been geared towards life issues. Nothing seemed to prepare us for working with those in the final stages of life where the issues are very different. A lot of our training had been about recognising and affirming a person's contribution, however small, but in the beginning we were hard pressed to get any contribution whatsoever. We had been taught to encourage choice and initiative, but how could we do that if a person fell asleep in the middle of a session? As idealistic, new drama therapists we were disheartened.

That was the beginning of us exploring other ways of interacting with our group. We realised that it was common for a resident to notice something we were wearing, especially if it was bright, so we made a point of wearing bright clothes and that gradually evolved into us bringing in bright swathes of fabric which we would use in the story. A square of bright blue lycra could be sky or sea or a dress or a train. My training emphasised the use of the imagination as an important tool. We discovered, however, that to someone with limited sight or failing mental abilities it could be confusing to be offered something that they could not actually experience with their senses. This is what prompted us to bring in objects that were related to the story and to show them around the group before the story. We were amazed to find that even very mundane objects were greeted with enthusiasm and would often prompt conversation and reminiscence. We realised that some people found it hard having so little of their familiar things around them and they relished looking at, touching and discussing the things we brought in. This did not mean that we did not ask people to use their imaginations at all. Paradoxically, it seemed people were more willing when their attention had been focused by a very real object and we learnt to remind someone if we saw there was some confusion 'we're pretending, it's in the story'.

Stories perform many functions in creative groupwork with elderly people. They provide an opportunity for active physical expression, engage the attention, raise the energy and interest level in the group, and allow alternative roles and relationships to be played out. Thus Lilian, who is in a wheelchair and almost deaf, plays the role of the healer woman and tends Frieda, the care assistant in her role as sick child. Michael plays Evening Star in a North American myth and has three nurses as his servants.

Folk tales from other cultures bring the world into the activities room and expand the horizons of people for whom they're rapidly closing down.

Stories are deliberately chosen to mirror and affirm the elderly person's experience. Stories that contain a central, elderly figure, that contain themes of loss and renewal, stories that contain characters taken for granted by the society in which they live but who receive their proper acknowledgement in the course of the story. Stories that provide plenty of opportunity for touch and, most important of all, contact with other human beings.

Because so many elderly people live in institutions or are separated from the extended family unit we can begin to relate to them as if they are a different species rather than the fruition of our own development. Stories are included from many other cultures to emphasise the universality of human experience as well as to provide a counterpoint to cultures where the view of old age is very negative.

In training other people to work with story and elderly groups, I have sometimes been greeted with scepticism and comments such as 'they wouldn't sit still for two minutes let alone listen to a story' or 'I don't think my residents would understand them'. These objections are often from those who work with people with dementia, a disease sometimes characterised by restlessness, poor concentration and mental confusion.

However, this is an area where I have done most of my work and repeatedly seen expectations like these confounded. I often describe my first experiences of trying to run a group which was made up of very frail, elderly people with dementia. It is important to point out that I did not run this group on my own but with another drama therapist. Our first session was chaotic to say the least. We had met our possible participants and they were all mobile. We spent a lot of time on our initial approach to people and escorting them into the room. Finally, we were all seated and we began to introduce ourselves. We used the session format we had developed in our work with other very frail elderly people, the use of objects related to the story, a very simple story, music from the 1940s. My experience in that first session was like trying to catch butterflies with a net that was full of holes. While my attention was taken up with one person, someone else was wandering out of the circle or gazing out of the room. I would ask a question of someone and they would answer what seemed like a completely different question. The change came when we abandoned the telling of the story prior to an enactment in favour of going straight on to enacting the story. As soon as there was something to watch, a physical focus, the attention of the group was caught, if only for a few moments – a disparate number of people became a group involved in an activity together. The level of involvement varied from person to person and sometimes from moment to moment. Hence the importance of a thread that carries through from the beginning of the session to the end. The person could phase out and in and the thread of the session was still there for him to return to. We discovered also over the next couple of sessions that attention could be trained once a convention had been established. It is like imagining a person who has never before encountered a TV. That person will not sit down meekly in front of it and watch its flickering images and detect the narrative thread that is unfolding on the screen. He would have to be taught to do that.

We discovered that quite quickly people began to respond to the convention of hearing a story. Heads would turn towards the speaker, eyes would focus on her face. There was more stillness in the room.

We learnt how to absorb peoples' comment into the fabric of the story.

When the group was very distracted we used what we had learnt in that initial session and moved on to telling the story and enacting simultaneously.

We began to develop relationships with people in the group. When we arrived on a Wednesday morning some would drift over to greet us while others smiled and waved from their seats.

The staff on the wing began to comment on changes they had noticed in residents after the session. Lily had been previously very aggressive to other residents, but she seemed calmer and less agitated after the session. Gill had not spoken for days and walked with her hands clutched around her sides, balled into fists. She left the session on Alison's arm, her head inclined towards her, deep in conversation. Bertha had had to be wheeled into the session. She had collapsed on the care assistant when she was walking her in.

She had been very tearful in the session, putting her head in her hands and wailing. As co-leader for that session I was able to sit beside her and hold her hand and listen to her distress. The story focused her attention outside of herself and she began to interact with the others and smile and laugh a little. When she left she walked with me back to her seat. She was frail but not unsteady, the way she had been.

The therapeutic use of story

The oral tradition precedes books as the primary source of education and entertainment and in some parts of the world still exists as such.

Stories are used with children to show them how to be in the world, to give them an idea of an ethical code, and to encourage them to put themselves in another person's shoes, that is, to cultivate empathy.

One of the first misconceptions I usually address when teaching people who do not come from a therapeutic background how to use story is the one that says stories are just for kids. This is particularly important when training in the elderly care field, where there is a very understandable sensitivity towards avoiding infantilising grown adults. One of the ways in which I deal with this is to get people to think about how much we are surrounded and fascinated by stories in our adult, contemporary lives, from the newspaper reports that absorb us to the soap operas we watch avidly the world over. Even the most succinct of art forms, the advert, has caught on to the power of story.

About the stories in this book

The stories in this book are traditional stories from different parts of the world, and all ones I have personally used with elderly groups and individuals.

They include myths, wonder tales, folk tales and fairy stories, from North America, Africa, Russia, Europe and China. Although the cultures from which the stories originate may appear very different, the underlying recurring themes are similar. The stories explore such themes as, `How can I have a happy life?', `What is an ethical way to live?' and `What happens when we die?' So many of the older people we work with know the answers to these questions. As an ancient maxim in Swaziland says: 'What an old man can see sitting down, a young man cannot see standing up'.

I

Why Groups?

In this chapter I am going to talk about why group activities are important in work with older people, the aims of group activities and what opportunities they can give us for improving the quality of life for all involved – staff and clients. I am also going to talk about how important it is that people choose whether they want to become involved or not, their level of involvement, and how to encourage and facilitate people's involvement in, and enjoyment of, the group.

One of the first things to appreciate is that groups are potentially very scary for all of us. Most people have mixed feelings towards being in a group, particularly a new one. Our first experience of groups was likely to have been our family of origin, which may have been a warm, safe environment or one fraught with conflict. Being in a group may evoke memories or unconscious associations with our family of origin which may or may not be pleasant. On the other hand, if the group we set up is relaxed and informal, encourages laughter, respects differences and values the individual, it can go a long way to resolving pain from the past and become a potentially healing experience.

From play group or our very first days of school onwards, we were exposed to a much wider variety of people, and the experiences we had influence the way we feel about groups, particularly ones with which we are not familiar. Our expectations may be of fun and positive experiences and we can also fear humiliation and the possibility of not fitting in. I have heard people say of an elderly person, 'oh, she's fine one to one but she never wants to do anything in a group', as if this were a very peculiar thing rather than the reality for lots of people. The prospect of participating in a new group often raises anxiety levels.

One of the ways I explore this in training groups is to ask people what thoughts and feelings they have about starting the group. I ask them to think of what hopes and fears they have for the training group and for the purposes of this exercise I ask them to focus on their fears. Often people's fears on coming to a new training group are strikingly similar. Examples include fearing they are going to be asked to do something they're uncomfortable with and they won't be able to say no, fearing they will be humiliated and fear of looking foolish, particularly in front of colleagues or someone they know.

I then ask people to consider that these may be the fears of some of the elderly people they are inviting to their activity groups. I also ask people to think about what they know about the elderly people they are wanting to involve and use that information to imagine other anxieties they may have. For example, we can begin to realise that for someone whose hearing is failing and who cannot keep up with a group discussion, a group activity may hold some anxiety. This is also the case for someone whose mobility is limited and, who is worried in case demands are going to be made which some members of the group can meet but he or she very publicly cannot, or someone whose memory is going and who is doing their best to cover it up. In this way we begin to develop much more sensitivity towards the needs of individual group members and thus organise ourselves accordingly. It also helps to give a more realistic picture of why some people refuse to come to groups and help us to reassure them accordingly.

Aims in organising a group

So why would we want to organise a group for elderly people? There are many good reasons for organising a group or some kind of recreational activity for an older person. In the move away from the medical model of caring for a person's physical needs towards a more holistic and person-centred approach which includes emotional and social needs, activities offer all kinds of opportunities.

Here are some of the aims:

- contact and relationship building
- providing an experience of community for people who may be feeling very isolated
- enjoyment
- self-esteem
- a reduction in boredom and an increase in interest

- providing an ideal opportunity for the practise of the person-centred approach
- maintaining and extending people's physical and mental abilities.

The first area I am going to look at is one that applies equally in our day-to-day work with people but activities allow us to focus on it without the demands of other practical considerations. This is where we place the focus of the activity on the quality of the contact between people. When this becomes our focus all the other aims mentioned above are automatically or more easily facilitated.

Contact and connection

'Contact' and 'connection' are very specific terms used to describe types of interactions between people.

Contact is about relating to someone on a personal level. It is emotional openness and physical closeness. It is reciprocated – in other words, I cannot make contact with you if you do not wish to make contact with me. I make contact with my eyes, my voice and my touch. I can only make contact with one person at a time. It is a very one-on-one interaction.

One of the ways of understanding contact is to look at the experience of infants. Apart from mother, with whom they have enjoyed, and hopefully continue to enjoy, the closest of bonds, tiny babies are surrounded by people they don't know. They come into a world full of strangers. They are non-verbal. They have no concept of time or place. They are doubly incontinent and they can't even support the weight of their own head. They are completely helpless and dependent on others for their very survival. They have to know they are safe and can trust the people around them but they have no understanding of the language. How we communicate that information to them is in the way we hold them, the way we speak to them and the eye contact we make with them. I would like you to take a few minutes to think about the elderly people you work with in relation to the picture I have painted above. If you are working with very 'youthful' elderly people, similarities may not be striking. However, if you are working with very frail elderly people, particularly those who are dementing, there may be a lot of features you recognise. This is what I refer to as the links between a pre- and post-verbal stage, and it is useful to see the ways in which we bond with people in these stages.

Experiments carried out in the 1970s (Harlow and Suomi 1970) showed what happens when these crucial elements of touch, eye contact and vocal tone are denied to the infant. In these experiments new born babies were bathed and fed and changed, but they were not cuddled or talked to and no eye contact was made with them. The babies began by being very distressed, then they became very withdrawn and eventually they deteriorated rapidly in what was termed 'failure to thrive'. Failure to thrive means that all the growth and development of the baby stops on every level: physically, emotionally, mentally and socially. Basically, what was being explored here was the way human beings bond. However, it is not only when we are tiny and dependent on others that we need to be looked at and talked to and held – throughout our lives we have these needs. What happens is that as soon as we develop a degree of autonomy we can seek to satisfy these needs according to our own personal make-up and whoever is available (many is the time a grandparent or a family friend becomes the most reliable source of contact if the mother is lacking). As people get older and for whatever reason lose their independence, that desire and need for contact is still there but the opportunities for getting those needs met may be fewer. The person confined to their house and visited by the home help once a day may have her as their only source of contact. Little wonder, then, that the most common problem I hear when I train home helps is their client's dependency on them, to the extent often that they will not tolerate a substitute even when their regular person is on holiday. The person in a rest home may be surrounded by people but feel very lonely because no one is bothering to make contact.

Our self-esteem is built and maintained by the quality of the contact we have with others. We get much of the way we think about ourselves from the response of other people towards us. If other people avoid touching us, or when they do they do so in a very perfunctory way, we can begin to recoil from our own skin and find ourselves objects of distaste. If no one looks us in the eye we will begin to doubt our own existence. If no one speaks to us, or when they do they use a very harsh vocal tone, we will begin to feel afraid. This is true for all of us but particularly the elderly person who through circumstances has become very dependent on the support of others. How much more frightening their experience must be.

Making links between those poles of the developmental scale, the very young and the very old, is often taboo in the field of elderly care, yet I think there are some very useful lessons to be learned by doing so. One of the reasons I do make links between old age and infancy is that I want to encourage people to identify with the elderly person and not pathologise them or see them as someone alien to themselves. This is particularly relevant when working with people whose behaviour may sometimes appear bizarre, for example the elderly person with a dementing illness. So I emphasise the fact that we are all at different stages of development, with infants at one end and the very elderly at the other, and that as humans we make contact in very similar ways. There are some cultural differences and if you are working with people from a different cultural background you need to check the appropriate behaviour. I have trained African staff who told me that in their country it was considered disrespectful to make direct eye contact with an older person.

If there is an injunction in elderly care not to acknowledge similarities between infancy and old age we need to examine what the specifics of the situation are. One of the residential homes I know instructed staff not to hold the hands of residents when they accompanied them anywhere. The thinking behind this was that we only ever hold the hands of children. One of the major ways we get information about a person and their attitude towards us is how they touch us. This injunction deprived the elderly people of this information as well as the other obvious benefits of touch. It also ignored the commonplace reality which was that it was the residents themselves who reached for the staff member's hand. It was their choice and initiative, two things we are striving to encourage!

Contact is how we bond with another person and it is reciprocated, so that in allowing a person to make contact with us we allow ourselves to be touched by them on an emotional level. This is so important when working with an elderly person who may be rapidly losing their physical abilities as well as their mental abilities. Their emotional self may be very much more intact and this is the level we need to work on. The challenge of working with older people in an emotionally open way is that it is likely to produce a variety of feelings. We may grieve when the person dies, and the image of the ailing older person with diminishing powers may evoke fears for our own old age. The important thing is to be aware of these feelings and, if possible, talk about them with colleagues.

Contact is a one-to-one interaction. If we return to the image of the infant – if one parent is cuddling the child, looking at it, talking to it, and the other parent wants to have some contact with it, it is necessary for the first parent to move back, to break the contact so that the second parent can move in and establish contact. This is very important to remember when you are running groups. Our primary communication was one to one, so if we provide opportunities for this within a group activity we can sustain people's interest and focus for longer and give them a more satisfying experience.

The liberating thing about contact is that it does not depend on cognitive ability. This can be very heartening in the case of a dementing illness or after a stroke, where the brain and cognitive functions, including speech and orientation, can be affected to a quite major degree. People can start assuming that communication with that person is now impossible, but remember we make contact through the skin, the ears and the eyes – in other words using touch, vocal tone and eye contact. Words are not a part of this except in so far as they easily carry our vocal tone. Verbal incomprehension is not a bar to contact.

Information about contact can influence the way we work. It can influence the way we organise ourselves physically in relation to the client. If we want to be able to see each other's face as clearly as possible, be within easy touching distance and to hear each other's vocal tone, we need to position ourselves in front of the person and on their level. This can often mean crouching down but this is so much more preferable than standing and leaning over someone. In a crouching position we will be slightly below the person who is sitting. This means they do not have to strain their neck to make eye contact with us. It also puts them in a more powerful position and makes us very accessible to being touched. From here we can lean forward if the person is very hard of hearing. In these ways we adapt our behaviour in order to communicate and make contact rather than demanding that the other person adapt (which they are often not in a position to do) in order to communicate with us.

Connection is more about social interaction based on role. It is necessarily more distant, although it can be friendly. We will in all probability have more connection interactions than contact interactions, and this makes sense as there is only so much intimacy we can sustain in our lives. Both are equally vital. What may happen in the lives of elderly people, however, is that they may have plenty of connections but not enough contact, and this is a need we would do well to address.

A example of this could be the care worker who is helping someone eat. They may be sitting quite close with their arm around the back of the person's chair. Their attention, however, is elsewhere. They may be talking to one of the other workers. They may be thinking about all the other things they have to get done in the course of the day. There is connection here but no contact. A different scenario is the worker sitting opposite the person, making eye contact and talking to them, holding a hand or stroking their arm. Contact is there. Now it may be that the reality of the work situation makes it well nigh impossible to give this degree of attention to everybody all of the time. We need to set up more ideal situations where this contact can happen and make it a conscious aim.

I have seen a lot of connection interactions and relationships in elderly care, and some are useful and mutually beneficial. The drawback is when that is the only interaction available, when the staff refuse to drop their role of professional care giver or expert or whatever, in order to have a person-to-person interaction with their clients or residents. This refusal may be more about not having a model of care available that allows a movement between closeness and distance. The concepts of contact and connection provide this model. There are going to be times when the most appropriate response to a person involves being emotionally open – when someone is very distressed, for example. There are also going to be times when we need to move into role and distance ourselves. The challenge is to develop enough flexibility to be able to do both rather than be fixed in one position or the other.

An important part of both contact and connection is communication, and this is the area where I am most often asked to train. The definition of communication I use in training is as follows: communication is the means by which I express my thoughts, feelings, fears, hopes, aspirations, preferences, opinions and so on; in other words, who I am. The means I use to do this include words, vocal tone, facial expression, eye contact, body language, gesture and touch.

As you can see, words are only one part of a communication spectrum. Research (Mehrabian 1971) has shown that they constitute only 7 per cent of our communication. The other 93 per cent is made up of other elements in the spectrum. All of these elements should blend together so that what we are saying, the words, match how we are saying it. If they don't, we will tend to believe the vocal tone and the body language rather than the words. It's not what you say but how you say it that's important. In this way, if someone is lying to us, we can usually pick it up on some level. We may not be able to put our finger on what is wrong but we will feel confusion. This is a really important point to remember when working with people (especially people who may be experiencing some confusion anyway). It is vital that we are congruent – that is, what is being presented on the outside matches what is going on inside. If someone asks you if you are well today and you're not, don't try to smile brightly and say, 'yes, thank you, I've never felt better'. Your words may be saying one thing but everything else about you will be saying the opposite, which is very confusing. Some staff find this a difficult concept and say, 'but I don't want to burden my residents, they have enough problems of their own'. You are not burdening someone if you say, 'thanks for asking Lily, and I feel really awful today, I think I might be going down with something'. This puts the client in the picture, it makes it clear that it has nothing to do with her, and it gives her the opportunity to show concern and care for you rather than it always being the other way round.

The most expressive woman I ever worked with had a dementia and was completely dysphasic. Yet communicating with her was a joy, she was so clear. If she was angry she would gesture wildly, she frowned and spat out her words. The words were incomprehensible to me but her emotional tone was unmistakable. If she asked a question her intonation went right up at the end of 'sentences'; she smiled and turned her head slightly to one side. When she was miserable her shoulders drooped, she avoided eye contact and the vitality went out of her voice – she was often on the brink of tears. In each case I had no idea of the details of what she was saying but it didn't matter and it was no bar to responding to her on an emotional level.

The group as opportunity for sharing and community

Having said that the prospect of a group raises anxiety levels, it is also important to remember that some people actively relish the experience of being in a group. I ran a group in a day centre where people were used to being in communal activities and were very outgoing. In a group people get the chance to share their energy, the brighter members can lift the spirits of the more withdrawn. A group can become an opportunity for sharing and community. As a person gets older the amount of social interaction available begins to diminish. If one becomes disabled or housebound one may only see one or two people a day and never see fresh faces. If for some reason we go into a hospital or residential home we may be exposed to a lot more people, not just the other residents but the care staff, volunteers, domestic staff, secretaries and administrators. However, if our mobility is restricted, for example after a stroke, or we are very depressed we may never leave our room. And then there are the effects of illness, particularly dementia. The first time I visited a secure, long-stay ward for elderly people with dementia, I was struck by the isolation and the lack of contact between people. Several people wandered, seemingly in their own world. Others were sitting next to each other on a sofa but seemed to have little awareness that another person was there. Some residents were sitting neatly in chairs. Some slumped asleep, some sat bolt upright with their handbags in their laps as if waiting to go home. It seemed to me that anything that could ease that isolation would make a tremendous difference to people's lives.

Enjoyment

A group can be so stimulating and exciting, bringing us into contact with a variety of different people and personalities. Research (Cousins 1989) into why happy people live longer has discovered a group of life-enhancing chemicals which are triggered by peals of laughter. Never underestimate the power of laughter and having fun. Laughter is also infectious. There is no better publicity for your group than people coming out looking and sounding as if they have had a really good time. What is not so obvious is how the fun element can be used to stimulate and extend people in a way that is not testing or a chore. A group can provide the space within which to play, and activities which emphasise the importance of play and playfulness over product are much more appropriate for this client group. Product-based activities are about producing or doing something and the elderly person is in the position of perhaps not being able to do things that in the past he took for granted. The older and more disabled the person, the more marked this becomes. Playfulness is much more about 'being' while at the same time leaving space for spontaneity and creativity.

Self-esteem

A group can be used to build self-esteem. We can make a point of affirming each person's contribution and provide an atmosphere of encouragement in which people thrive. We can aim to balance the prevailing attitudes of negativity towards older people with an emphasis on what people can do rather than what they cannot. People then begin to blossom, feeling confident and relaxed enough to take risks and reveal more about themselves.

In one of the youthful elderly groups I ran, there was a man who was teased at the day centre because he prided himself on being intellectual and well read – this was interpreted by others, both staff and members, as arrogance. I was warned 'not to let him take over the group'. The problem was that the very qualities that this man prized in himself the community he was a part of undervalued, so the more he tried to get acknowledgement from the group the more people saw him as self-aggrandising. On top of this he was aware of disrespectful things that were said about him and would retaliate by insulting the intellectual abilities of the other members. One of the things the story group gave him was plenty of intellectual stimulation in the form of the stories and the themes and questions they provoked. Also, the group enacted the stories and Jack was a very skilled and enthusiastic role player. As one of only two men in a group of women he was often called on to play a major role in the sessions. He got to show a side of himself that was very fun and humourous and he developed a different relationship with some of the other women in the group which spilled over and improved their contact outside.

Reducing boredom and increasing interest

It is often underestimated how boring and lacking in stimulation the lives of a lot of elderly people can be. When people think of stress it is often the stress of having too much to do and being overstimulated. This is what is known as 'overload stress'. However, there is another aspect of stress which is the stress of the long-term unemployed and the parent at home all day with small children, which is known as 'underload stress'. One of the ways I explore this aspect in training is to ask people to make a list of everything they've done in the last twenty-four hours. Then I ask them to compare it with the average day in the life of one of their clients. One can begin to see how restricted and lacking in variety older person's lives can be. Often behaviours seen as challenging, such as wandering or aggressive outbursts, have their origin in boredom.

Maintaining and extending people's physical and mental abilities

Another reason people give for the importance of activities is the need to stimulate and encourage elderly people so that they retain as many skills as possible for as long as possible. I would certainly agree with the notion that a person who sits around all day doing very little and perhaps having things done for them will quite quickly become more and more disabled, both mentally and physically. However, it is the approach that you take towards achieving this aim that is important.

If you place the emphasis on fun, building self-esteem and providing opportunities for contact, people will loosen up, relax and begin to extend themselves without even thinking about it.

You can often tell what approach is being taken with a group just from observing the body language of the group members and the facilitators. I once visited a day hospital for older people who were in the early stages of dementia. The manager really wanted the clients to retain as much of their faculties as they could for as long as possible. There is nothing wrong with this as an aim. It's just the way that you go about it. The ways she had devised to do this were very testing and confronting for the clients. The activity I observed was one where pictorial images had been made which gave clues to a particular song which the group had to guess. Once the group had guessed the song they then had to sing it. What I observed from looking at the group was that most were sitting right back in their chairs holding themselves very rigidly. There were no smiles or laughter. The group leaders were sitting forward and singing most of the words of the songs – they were obviously straining to involve the clients, but apart from a couple who were singing along quite happily most clients looked distinctly uncomfortable and tense. The activity involved two sophisticated tasks. The first was to recognise the images and link them to the name of a song. The second was to remember the melody and words of the song.

The absence of smiling and laughter is a very clear sign. The staff were ignoring the information they were getting from the group in terms of their resistance to the activity and the information they were getting from their own experience that it felt like really hard work. Perhaps it was seen as an opportunity to praise those who did remember the words, but what about those who didn't and those who remembered the words last week but can't remember them this week? The exercise by its nature tests the part of the person most affected by the dementia, the cognitive abilities. The group members were in the early stages of dementia, when a lot of people have awareness that they are beginning to lose their faculties. This exercise could have been a very clear and painful example of this.

So what other ways are there to help people to retain their faculties for as long as possible? The following guidelines may be of use:

1. Take away the idea of a test. Very few of us perform well in testing conditions.

2. Take the emphasis off the goal being to get the person to *do* something, whether that is to remember the words of a song or to throw and catch a ball, and change it to providing opportunities

for contact and developing the relationship between the two of you.

3. Make the exercise fun and encourage laughter.

4. Notice and affirm people's contribution so they are encouraged to put out more without fear of ridicule or being found publicly to be lacking.

With this approach we will leave pleasant associations in the mind which the person will want to repeat in the future. We also save ourselves a lot of frustration and tiredness. It is exhausting to try and get people to do something they don't really want to do. This process is also very paradoxical because most people perform better in an atmosphere of affection and laughter and playfulness. So we may very well find that once the emphasis is changed people start doing the most amazing things – although it may have been that they were doing them all the time; it's just we were so busy trying to get a result we didn't notice. Testing, no matter how subtle, just serves to increase people's anxiety levels even further.

Activities as an opportunity to use the person-centred approach

The 'person-centred approach' as a term was coined by Carl Rogers, a leading exponent of humanistic psychotherapy. It has since been adopted by the Dementia Research Project in Bradford and is used to describe an overall approach to dementia care. It places the emphasis on the person and not on the disease.

The definition I use in training is as follows: the person-centred approach involves treating a person as an individual with rights and preferences, thoughts and feelings, offering choice and opportunities for initiative wherever possible. It involves bearing in mind our own thoughts and feelings, in other words treating ourselves as a person.

As a principle it is relatively easy to understand. However, it is much more difficult to practise. This is one reason why activity time is so important. If I place the focus on making contact with the person and I leave time to do that, then the process becomes a lot more satisfying for both of us.

Choice

Offering and supporting people's choice is an important part of the person-centred approach. Choice is like a muscle: the more we get to exercise it the stronger it grows. The converse is also true – the more choice is taken away and decisions made for us, the more disabled and apathetic we become. It is often much easier and quicker to make decisions on other people's behalf and sometimes this may be unavoidable. However, if someone has not been given a lot of choice they lose the ability and become reluctant to make a choice when it is presented to them. I have heard a lot of people say, 'she won't choose between tea or coffee', as if there is no point in offering a choice if the person won't make what seems like a very simple one (I worked in one hospital where people weren't even given this choice – tea time brought cups of sugared coffee). Again this is where activity time is so important. In story sessions I have seen people readily make imaginative choices. I have asked, 'do you think the girl should marry the farmer's son or go on the journey?' or, 'should the villagers open the box they promised to keep closed or not?'. Stories are a really useful means of eliciting choice as they encourage an emotional response, and because they are theoretical they have no consequences.

The most common complaint I have heard from people organising and running groups for very elderly and/or frail individuals is, 'I ask loads of people but no one wants to come'. This can result in a number of things. One is that any attempt at activities is abandoned (although the notice board or day book would give the impression there is a lot going on). Alternatively, activities are organised and people are compelled to come via a variety of means from bribery ('go to the group and I will give you a cigarette') to seduction ('please come to the group, for me, please') to actually physically wheeling someone in their wheelchair or not even asking them if they want to come. It is so important that people choose to be part of the group, and when they do you have a completely different atmosphere to one where people have been coerced in subtle and not so subtle ways.

I trained in a residential home where one gentleman came to a story session because he had been told it was an opportunity to air grievances he had about the home. Can you imagine living somewhere where the people who are responsible for looking after you misinform you in this way? It doesn't just have repercussions for the session, it affects a person's sense of trust and safety.

So what happens if you have devised a wonderful activities programme and no one wants to come or, as is often the case, you get the same, more able people coming every time but not the quieter, frailer types? How can you encourage a range of different people to come?

Youthful elderly people are much more likely to choose an activity on the basis of what is being offered, for example a quiz rather than a dancing session. As people get older, particularly if they are very frail, hard of hearing or dementing, they are much more likely to respond to the person who is asking them, in other words contact. If I do not understand what is being said to me but I feel I can trust you and you are not rushing me or coercing me, I will probably want to go with you no matter what is on offer. It will help for me to know that I will not have to do anything if I don't want to, that it is my company that is being sought. I may need reassurance that I can leave if I want to. If I decide I don't want to come I don't want to be made to feel bad about what is my decision. I may also appreciate knowing that my saying no this time does not mitigate against my being asked the next time. In this way we support people's choices and leave doors open for them to step through whenever they feel ready.

We all need to work up to things. It's a very rare person who can switch from one mode of being to another effortlessly. We need a little help, and an acknowledgement that transitions from one place to another, either literal or emotional, can be difficult. As I've said, it's really important to realise that group situations are potentially stressful, so we need to think about where people are coming from and think of ways to smooth their transition. I've heard people saying, 'Frank's been sitting in his room all day, he must be so bored, he'll come to a group'. Frank may be bored but the transition from his solitary state to one where there are lots of people and possibly demands being made on him, from his own room to a communal area, is too big a leap for him to contemplate without help. This help can take a variety of forms. The most obvious is that if Frank has been on his own all day, one-to-one contact is going to be the next logical step for him. He may need reassurance and information. So, for example, remind Frank who is going to be there, mention the people you know he likes, remind him he doesn't have to do anything, he can just be a member of the group. If you know he likes stories, talk to him about the story. If you know he likes the objects, tell him about them. This may all take time but it is part of the session – it is contact and relationship building and what the work is all about. Frank may still decide he doesn't want to come and that is fine. Acknowledge his choice and tell him you will ask him again next time, and make sure you do.

This kind of approach, as long as it is consistent, will build up trust towards you which is essential for working with any group of people, but especially with elderly people where it may be a rare commodity.

I trained in a day centre where there was choice around which group you wanted to be in, but unfortunately no provision was made for those who didn't want to be in a group but wanted to sit and read or just chat. All the staff were needed to run the group activities and none of the clients could be left unsupervised. Here I advised the staff to acknowledge the difficulty of the situation and really emphasise to people that although they had to be in a group they could choose their own level of involvement and didn't have to do anything if they didn't want to.

Initiative

The types of initiative a very elderly person makes are often very subtle and we need to be observant to spot them and nurture them as we would a small plant – we also have to be working within a structure flexible enough to accommodate a piece of initiative that perhaps doesn't fit in with exactly what we planned for the session and feel confident enough to go with it.

Respecting the individual

The essence of the person-centred approach is a respect for the individual. The length of a person's attention span varies enormously. The optimum concentration span is twenty minutes, so for someone who is very tired or ill it is proportionately less. The advantage of a group, however, is that when someone reaches their personal optimum concentration span they can phase out and either have a rest or mentally process what's gone on in the group so far. The group will carry on as we don't all phase out at the same time. The person can phase back in when they are ready or if there is a change in tempo or whatever.

One of the groups of people who have traditionally been thought to have a very short attention span and therefore very difficult to involve in group activities is elderly people with a dementing illness. Dementia affects a person's ability to think, so it may be very difficult for them consciously to focus their attention. They may have extreme anxiety which makes it almost impossible to sit still for any length of time. Thus we must respect individual differences and develop a more inclusive way of working. If someone is very anxious and restless we don't have to insist they sit in the circle with everyone else if they find that difficult. They may need to wander around the room or even go and sit a little way off from the rest of the group. We can carry on treating them like the other members of the group – addressing comments to them, offering to show them things of interest, checking that they are alright: in other words including them in the group.

We need to respect individual contributions and different levels of involvement. Sometimes staff have very unrealistic expectations of what involvement in a group means. The expectation is that we all involve ourselves to the same extent or that we all need to be doing something all of the time. I find it very helpful when I am training in groups to point out that even in our training group people are making different contributions. Some people are very comfortable taking space in a group, some people are ideas people, some people operate best in pairs. We need different kinds of people to have a rich and varied group experience. Just because someone likes to sit and watch does not mean they are not contributing to the group.

Respecting the individual means you can adapt the format accordingly rather than expect people to adapt to fit the format. It can be so liberating for both parties and the effect of such flexibility is sometimes paradoxical – the less we are expected to perform, the lower our level of anxiety; the more relaxed we are the more likely we are to be creative. It also leaves space to be surprised by a client's contribution. When we are not so fixed on achieving a goal we can tune in more to the individuals in the group and spot the examples of initiative when they appear.

References

Cousins, N. (1989) *Head First: The Biology of Hope.* New York: Dutton.

Harlow, H.F. and Suomi, S.J. (1970) 'Nature of love – simplified', *American Psychologist, 25.*

Mehrabian, A. (1971) *Silent Messages.* California: Wadsworth.

2

The Story Session

Before you start there are some practical considerations that you may want to think about:

- Make sure the person has their glasses, hearing aid, walking frame or whatever else they need in order to get as much from the session as possible.

- Because you are trying to facilitate communication and concentration be aware of things that can interfere with that, for example the TV or radio.

- If you are in a position to choose the room in which to work, choose one where you can be undisturbed, preferably not the residents' sitting room (so other residents are not deprived of their communal space) and definitely not a thoroughfare.

- Easy access for all is important – allocate more time to taking people in wheelchairs up and down lifts, and so on. Remember it is not always a drawback if people have to be transported or escorted elsewhere (as long as it is not too far). Never underestimate how refreshing it can be for someone whose mobility is limited to have a change of scene.

- Temperature – if the room is too hot and stuffy (usually the case) people will doze; if it's too cold people will be uncomfortable and want to leave.

- Whenever possible make sure your activity doesn't clash with other pleasurable activities, such as a visit to the hairdresser or from a relative. We are trying to improve people's quality of life, so the more things there are to look forward to the better.

Make it clear that the sessions are not to be disturbed and be prepared to maintain that boundary. I once trained in a residential home where a member of staff came to collect a member of the group right in the middle of a session. The doctor had arrived for his weekly visit and this lady was on the list of people due to go and see him. Immediately the lady's concentration was broken and with it the focused calm in the group (this group was made up of a group of residents with dementia). I pleaded for five minutes so this woman could finish what she was doing and have some sense of completion rather than just rushing off. The staff member told me the woman would probably have to wait ages for the doctor anyway, as it was common practice to assemble all the residents who were to see him on any particular visit and he would work through them. Often residents waited for over an hour. In other words there was no rush.

In other cases, staff I don't know have come into sessions, leant over the backs of people's chairs and said things such as, 'do they understand what's going on then?'. Not only is this very distracting for the group (and you may have worked very hard to get their attention in the first place), but it is very disrespectful to both you and members of the group. If someone is keen to see what is going on in the group (and hopefully there will be a real excitement in the place because the group is going so well), invite them to join in as a member of the group but take time to talk to them about what the aims of the group are.

On the whole I would recommend you work to keep the sessions free of interruptions but always be flexible. In one of the places where I worked for many years the story session coincided with coffee break. I knew that coffee was the highlight of the morning for many of the residents and if they did not have it at the same time as everyone else they would miss out altogether, so it was one interruption we worked hard to incorporate no matter what time it arrived.

I've worked in places that were open plan so people were wandering in and out all the time. In these cases you have to work really hard to maintain your own concentration and focus the group on what is happening in the session.

I also worked in one residential home where the only place for the group was in the communal living room. This meant that those who wanted to join the session formed a circle in the middle of the room while the other people sat in chairs on the periphery of the room. This actually worked really well because what eventually happened was that there was an inner circle of people taking a very active part in the session, and an outer circle made up of people watching and throwing in suggestions and comments. Sometimes someone from the outer circle would become involved in the action of the inner circle. These sessions were greatly enhanced by the support of the staff.

Assistance in running the group

I ran a very able elderly group for years on my own and they were a group who were very vocal, energetic and used to being in groups. My job was much more about containing them and making sure everyone had their say than trying to stimulate a group with a much lower level of energy. However, this was the exception rather than the rule. Most of the groups I have worked with have been very frail and I relied very much on the support of staff.

I always recommend you work with another person, especially if the group is frail or disabled or dementing. If you are making opportunities for contact your goal, you will find yourself terribly split between the needs of different members of the group. When you are responsible for the direction the group is taking and maintaining the thread of the session to guide you through, it is really useful to have another person there. The other person can sit beside someone who is feeling very delicate, offer to play a part with someone if they would like to play it but feel unable to do so on their own, summon assistance outside the room to help someone to the loo and spot things that you might miss. It takes a lot of energy to run the kind of group I am describing, so having another person to help is invaluable. I would recommend this for any activity involving frail, elderly people, not just a storymaking one.

I have had the assistance of some wonderful people who have needed very little guidance from me and others who needed to be given, very diplomatically and with a light touch, information to enable them to work within the aims of the group. It is really important to recognise the value of people offering to help and you can have great support. I worked in a hospital where the activities organiser helped me in every single session. He was a great favourite with the residents and was a very humourous and witty man. In the beginning, however, he would often make comments that were very contemporary, making jokes about Margaret Thatcher in a story session, for example. This was sometimes jarring as it ran counter to what we were creating which was a magical world, part of whose charm (and therapeutic value) was that it was very distant and divorced from the contemporary world. After working together a while, I talked to him about it and he explained that initially he had felt a bit uncomfortable in the sessions and he used humour to cover up his discomfort. His style with the residents had always been very jokey and at first he found it difficult to find another way of being. After our discussion he was able to relax and enter into the spirit of the sessions a lot more.

Again, this way of working may be unfamiliar to a lot of the people who work in the establishment and sometimes we will need to spend time talking about and explaining what we are aiming to do. I have also come across people who were very good-willed and wanted to help, but were so controlling with the clients that they ran counter to everything we were trying to achieve. In such cases you have to weigh up whether it is worth having them assist you in the running of the group.

The make-up of a group

The ideal type of group allows for a whole range of people and is a way of involving those who don't normally get involved and who are perhaps very quiet and withdrawn. It's always helpful to have one or two people for whom this way of working comes very naturally and who welcome an opportunity to perform and be the centre of attention. It's also important to have people who like to sit and watch or whose contributions are a lot more low key. The most important prerequisite is that people have chosen to come.

You will of course have to 'take the temperature' of the group each time. This means tuning into the atmosphere on the ward or the wing and chatting to a few residents to see if what you're planning to do is appropriate for that particular day. People's moods can be very affected by a multitude of things – by the weather and time of year, illness or bereavement, staff and environmental changes. I've gone into places and changed what I've planned to do in favour of a much smaller group or two shorter groups, which has allowed more one-to-one contact. I've also had experience of what we used to call 'no' days. These were days when nobody seemed to want to do anything. Rather than get frustrated I would just have to accept it and not take it personally.

The format of a session

The format of a session influences how much a group enjoys and participates in the session. It can optimise people's input and ability to take in what is going on. This is very important in a group where you may have people with hearing loss, which makes it very difficult for them to take part in a group discussion, or someone with dementia whose concentration span is short and whose level of anxiety is very high, so that they find it difficult to sit still. Thus the format of the session should involve a combination of different elements that will hopefully appeal to a range of people and abilities. It should break up the time spent interacting in a big group and intersperse it with one-to-one interaction. The format I am detailing is designed for work with almost any group. Remember, the frailer the group, the more one-to-one contact is necessary in order to involve and include people. I use a five-fold format which looks like this:

- the approach
- the limber or warm-up
- the bridge – the use of objects
- the main event – the story
- the stabiliser.

The approach

One way of looking at the session is to see it as a movement from one-to-one interaction, which is about contact and closeness, to interacting with the wider group, which is more about connecting, and back again.

Hence approaching a person and asking them if they want to join the group is an example of one-to-one contact. Very often people can get very goal oriented when they set out to run a session and you might work in an environment that supports this. The goal is to get as many people as possible in a session in the shortest possible time. I have included the approach to the client as an invaluable part of the session so you allow enough time for it. It also means that if you are enlisting the help of other staff to assemble a group, you explain to them the importance of the approach and that people are given choices about whether they come or not.

People are then escorted into the space where you are going to run the session and seated in a circle or a semi-circle. Once you have everyone assembled in whatever way is most appropriate (a circle is a good shape for a group, allowing everyone to see each other and you to see everyone; however, this may not be ideal for a group of people in wheelchairs where you might find a semi-circle better. It's always worth experimenting with the shape to see what works best). We now have the beginnings of a group.

Depending on the type of group, one of you may have to stay in the room while the other goes to get other people. Otherwise people may wander off or go looking for one of you. You may want to play music that the group enjoys. Sometimes you may want to vary this to avoid boredom. At other times, you may decide that its familiarity serves as a cue to people whose memories are not so good, that it may evoke pleasant associations if the person cannot remember the exact nature of the activity.

Once you have everyone assembled, you can welcome everyone and make any announcements.

The limber or warm-up

The limber or warm-up takes place once the group has been gathered together, although there are some things that act as a warm-up even before everyone comes together in the room. These include things such as the music playing, essential oils burning or a comfortable, nicely decorated room. In this sense the warm-up is whatever makes the session or activity attractive and encourages the person to come.

Once you have your group present you begin with your limber or warm-up, which can take many forms and is appropriate to who you have in the group and whatever else may be going on at the time. It is really good at this point to have something that involves the group, gently raises the energy and focuses on a physical experience to ground people. One dementia group I had used to love throwing around a brightly coloured inflatable ball. This caused a lot of laughter and giggles and, as it stimulated reflexive actions, people's ability to throw and catch was not affected by the dementia. However, there were some days when the energy in the group was very low. On these days we would take round hand cream and help people to warm up their hands with a little gentle massage.

I have found that the use of the same or similar warm-up works well with particularly frail groups for whom repetition and familiarity may well be reassuring. You may want to try out a number of ideas and see what goes down well.

The aims of the limber are as follows:

- to provide opportunities for contact between individuals in the group
- to smooth the transition from whatever the person has been doing and help them adjust to a different environment with different

expectations, for example, someone who has been sitting in their room all day alone coming into a group

- to have fun, to relax people and thus encourage spontaneity and laughter
- to establish the ground rules of the group straight away, that is, that this is not a test
- to provide opportunities for choice and initiative.

Work on the same level as the group. In other words, if they are sitting down you sit down. Take your cue from the members. There may be people who stand up and you can affirm that but don't make it look as if everyone has to.

Choose an activity that encourages people to extend themselves without focusing on the activity itself, for example passing a ball around or stretching a piece of lycra between members of the group. This is particularly important with some people with dementia who have lost the ability to perform simple tasks through verbal incomprehension. The person is not physically unable, they just cannot make sense of the instruction. The way to deal with this is to encourage movement that is involuntary or reflexive, for example reaching to catch something.

Remember your aims, one of which is to affirm what people can do rather than what they cannot. Thus with people who have had a stroke and who have lost the use of one side of their body, I usually try and get them to focus on the side unaffected by the stroke. I don't want them to forget about the injured side, however, so I often encourage them to pat and stroke the injured side with the other hand. I have often seen people express contempt towards their limb that is paralysed, calling it useless and sometimes even hitting it. I think it's really important to intervene at this point, to stroke the limb gently and encourage the person to stroke it, to remind them how much their arm or leg needs looking after right now.

The bridge – the use of objects

The use of objects is an important feature of using story with an elderly group. Members of the group may be suffering some degree of sensory loss, usually, or at least more noticeably, hearing and/or sight, their energy levels may be very low, they may have had a stroke or be suffering from some other debilitating illness or they may be dementing and have very little short-term memory. The objects are used in order to make the experience of the story as rich as possible and appeal to as many different levels as possible. Thus the objects, usually two or three, are introduced after the limber and before the story or main event. You and your helper take the objects and show them to individuals and let them experience them in whatever way is appropriate for them. This could be talking about, feeling, holding, smelling or just looking at. It is amazing how much people enjoy this part of the activity.

The aims of using objects are:

- **to begin to introduce the story** – we are preparing the way for the telling of the story and want to build up as much interest as possible. It is also useful to have mentioned the story several times before the telling, perhaps when you approach the person asking them to come, maybe in the introduction to the session and definitely while examining the objects. This means that by the time you get to tell the story hopefully people are ready to listen. It can also be really important to tell people why you have brought the objects, 'because they are in the story' if there is some confusion. People may say, particularly in the early days of running the session, 'why are you showing me this?'. This is great because it gives you the chance to explain: for example, 'in the story the village is by the sea so I brought this sea shell in to have a look at'. You may also find that some people are reluctant to part with a particular object and it helps to be able to say, 'Can I have it back as we are going to need it in the story?'

- **to stimulate the senses** – objects are chosen on the basis of how relevant they are to the story but also how intriguing or stimulating they are to the senses. A feature of old age is a deterioration in the senses, but not all senses deteriorate at the same rate or to the same extent. Thus someone may be very deaf but have excellent eyesight or be poorly sighted but have a very strong sense of smell. Examples of objects I have used include swathes of brightly coloured material, which can represent anything you like – the sea or sunshine or a regal raiment – a fresh mango, which we discussed in the session, smelt, held and afterwards cut up and ate, and a bag of different hats which we tried on and admired

- **to raise the energy in the group** gently by being stimulating to the mind and provoking conversation. Depending on the group, an object can raise lots of questions, 'What is this box made of?

Where do you think it came from?'. This is definitely not about guessing correctly. The skill is to value people's contribution whatever the response.

- **to stimulate memory and provide new information about a person**. In a session where I brought a long length of fabric, one woman stood up and proceeded to measure the fabric expertly along her arm. She had been a seamstress in her youth but had not sewn for years. She was also one of the quietest members of the group and had never initiated anything before. The incident provided the opportunity to compliment her on her skill. She blushed and looked visibly delighted.

- **to provide an opportunity for one-to-one contact**. With contact the most ordinary object becomes fascinating, without it the most beautiful object loses its appeal. The important thing is that the objects are accompanied by a person. In the simplest way we can link the different members of the group by encouraging people to pass the object on to the person beside them rather than automatically passing it back to us. This is the area on which to focus if the person is not able to engage in a cerebral way and questions that emphasise mental abilities are not appropriate. You may just spend a few minutes with a person while she turns the object round and round in her hand. Sometimes people get a lot out of just holding an object and having some contact with another person.

- **to provide an opportunity to affirm the individual contribution and respect differences.** Thus I may hold up a piece of fabric and ask people what colour they would call it. Someone may say blue, someone may say brown. You have to resist the temptation to correct people. After all, most of us were educated in a system where that was the way we were assessed – on the basis of right or wrong. This is not about a right or a wrong answer. It is so liberating to be free of that and much more appropriate for work with a group of people who are losing the abilities they once took for granted and consequently may be very anxious about saying anything in a group for fear of 'getting it wrong'.

- **to ground the person in the here and now** if they are experiencing some confusion or are disassociating. If someone's attention has wandered and they have forgotten where they are or what they were doing, you can very gently draw their attention to an object which is very concrete and tangible. At the same time you can remind them of where they are.

GUIDELINES TO USING THE OBJECTS

It is certainly not necessary to spend a lot of money on objects, in fact quite the reverse. I've sent people away from training days with homework which consists of going home and choosing an object to bring in the following day to practise with. People have returned with a sponge from the bathroom, or an ornament from the bedroom, or a handful of rice from the kitchen. All these were objects that could have been used on their own or in a story session. People have often been amazed when I've brought in examples of objects I've used in sessions because piled in a heap they look like the leftovers from a jumble sale! Yet used in a session the object assumes a greater significance. Residents may have had strawberries for dessert at lunch and not given them a second thought. But one fresh strawberry linked to the story of Granny Greencoat and taken around so that individuals can smell it and exclaim at its redness suddenly becomes a different proposition entirely.

To avoid overloading people, limit the amount of objects to two or three. Ideally, there should only be as many objects as there are people to take them round. Choose objects that you feel excited about sharing with the group and have a personal significance for you. I would always return from holiday with souvenirs that became objects in stories. This was a way of involving people in my life and providing a sense of continuity.

Hold the object and invite the person to look at it or feel it. Do not place it automatically in the person's hand. If they reach for it eagerly, offer it to them to hold. Remember that if a person's sight is poor they may mistake what you are holding. I once had an old lady shriek when I showed her a shell. She thought it was a little animal. So watch the person carefully for any signs of confusion or alarm, particularly if they are not verbal. If the person shows any reluctance at all, move the object away. Do not force an object on anyone – you will destroy all the trust you are endeavouring to build up.

Sometimes an object is such a success with someone that they want to keep it or they become confused and think it is theirs. This happened to me a number of times. I once brought in some jewellery because there were jewels in the story. I encouraged people to try it on and then complimented them on how great they looked. It was only natural that one of the ladies formed a bit of attachment to the jewellery after that. I explained I needed the jewels for the story and could I use them for that, but she was adamant. They were her jewels and she was not going to take them off. Rather than upset her I let it go. Fortunately, it was costume jewellery and not a family heirloom so I wasn't too nonplused. Most of the time when people have wanted to hang on to an object they have lost interest in it or they have been quite happy to give it up by the end of a session so I have been able to retrieve it. This is preferable by far than wresting an object away from someone, which I would not recommend.

The main event – the story

The story forms the main event or focus of the session.

The aims of working with story are:

- to provide a thread or theme which can give focus to both the facilitator and participants

- to mirror and affirm the experience of individuals in the group for example, using stories that contain a central elderly figure, that include themes of loss and resolution

- to provide and encourage imaginative choices and initiatives

- to provide an opportunity for roles and varied relationships with staff which affirm the clients; for example a staff member may play a person who is sick and be looked after by one of the clients, which is a reversal of everyday roles and provides a different perspective for both parties

- to provide opportunities for contact within the group.

If you are not familiar with this way of working or have used story before but not with elderly groups, you may be finding it difficult to visualise what it's going to look like and how it could work with your particular client group. The most useful image I can think of to convey what it is like is the image of the pantomime or music hall. In panto there is a lot of interaction between the 'audience' and the 'performers'. In a story session we are working to involve our 'audience' in a variety of ways. This could be by asking their advice or having them enact a role. In panto there is a lot of repetition of phrases – 'oh, no, he isn't, oh, yes, he is!' – with an elderly group you may well have to repeat phrases or parts of the story for the benefit of the hard of hearing or confused. In panto, gesture and facial expression are exaggerated – the style is not at all naturalistic. We can lose people if we are too subtle and sophisticated in a story session where there may be poor eyesight. Both the story session and panto rely on simplicity of narrative to engage and retain the attention of the 'audience'. It also means there is more chance of actively involving the audience.

TELLING THE STORY

In telling the story what you are probably not going to be able to do is start at the beginning and go through to the end without stopping or physically moving. With an elderly group you have to be prepared to be much more flexible.

In a very able elderly group I used to tell the story to a semi-circle of people while sitting in one place. Everyone could hear and understand. They would often immediately start discussing the story once I had finished (and often before I had finished too!). When it came to casting the story people would nominate each other, so I had to encourage them to volunteer themselves which they then very readily did. I would narrate a simplified version of the story I had just told them and provide the minimum of prompting or leave it to one or two group members who had very good memories. I rarely played a role myself as the group included excellent and often hilarious improvisers. Those not playing roles were a very active audience, often calling out suggestions or making comments.

In a group of people who had all had strokes, most were in wheelchairs so we sat in a semi-circle and I would move around as I told the story as some had hearing problems. Staff assisting me played roles that were not taken by members of the group. Often I would cue an 'actor' by going over and touching their shoulder while reminding them of who they were in the enactment. This was particularly important in this group, where one of the key players was totally blind. I might say, 'so the king' (touching the person playing the king) 'said to his daughter, 'daughter it is time for you to marry'. The person could then repeat the phrase or improvise around it.

The basics of storytelling are:

1. *A love of the story.* I am going to be talking a lot more about choosing stories to suit our client group, but it is still very important that the story is one that we also love and feel some emotional connection to. One way to discover stories we like is

simply to read as many stories as we can and check out our response to them.

2. *A desire to share the story with others.* In the same way that one of the guidelines for choosing objects to share with residents was that they were objects that we ourselves enjoyed and felt stimulated by, so it is with stories. Have a regard for your listeners, treat them as friends. Share your pleasure in the stories with your friends.

3. *A working knowledge of the story.* Confidence comes with knowing your material. Take the time to learn the story and practise it often – in the car, to a friend, whenever. Just as the activity is not a test for the group it is not a test for you. No one is really going to mind if you get lost and have to refer to your notes now and again. Help yourself in the beginning by choosing simple stories that you have perhaps read several times before with other groups so you are familiar with them.

4. *Having the skills to tell the story.*

GENERAL POINTS OF STORYTELLING

1. You may begin by reading stories from a book. This is fine, especially in the beginning when you are building your confidence. If you are going to read a story mark the text in advance. Prepare yourself by reading it aloud before you try with a group. Learn to keep your head up while reading so that your mouth is towards the listeners even if your eyes are down.

2. As you gain in confidence try telling the stories by heart. This will give you so much more freedom. You will be able to make eye contact with people. You will notice who is having trouble concentrating and you can respond accordingly. If someone is looking confused you can clarify things for them or remind them this is a story. You can try to incorporate people's comments into the fabric of the story.

3. Speak as clearly as possible and don't rush. Learn to pause – this gives both you and the listener time to take the story in. Never forget to breathe. Rather than raise the volume of your voice throughout the story for the benefit of those who have difficulty hearing, which can be very wearing for both you and the other

members of the group, move closer to individual people, repeat certain phrases or have your assistant sit beside them and check they can hear. However, don't have the expectation that hearing the story is required for an enjoyment of the session. Sometimes people are happy just to sit and watch you and be a member of the group.

4. How you open and close the story is important – one engages the listener and the other gives a sense of completeness and satisfaction. You may start to involve people straight away by the judicious use of questions. I would often say what part of the world a story had come from and ask if anyone had ever been there.

5. Practise listening – the best storytellers are often the best listeners also. See if you can spot the storyteller on the bus, at a party or a family gathering and identify what it is they are doing that is making them an effective storyteller (this could be the way they pause, their use of gestures or the confident use of their voice). Watch for devices you can use yourself comfortably and unselfconsciously.

6. Remember all we've learnt about contact and connection and use it in your storytelling; in other words, eye contact, touch and vocal tone. Look around at people and try and make eye contact. Move around and gently touch people to get their attention. Use your voice in order to recapture people's attention. Suddenly vary the pitch or the volume to highlight a particularly dramatic moment.

CASTING THE STORY

You may need to devote a lot of time to going around the group asking who would like to play what. Remember the goal at this point is not to cast the story. If that was the case it would probably be easier and quicker to do all the parts yourself! The casting, like every other component of the session, is designed to provide opportunities for contact, for choice and initiative, for affirming people's strengths and abilities, for sharing and enjoyment. Giving choice means that people choose their part, they are not allocated one. If someone is non-verbal you may offer different parts and watch for the reaction, checking as you go that it is in line with the person's wishes. One of the most enthusiastic and charismatic role players I have known had had a stroke and was non-verbal. On his cue, he would throw his head back and sing. As the narrator I would 'translate' his singing into words, checking as I did so that my translation accurately conveyed what he wanted.

People do not have to get up and move around to play a part. They do not have to speak. The important thing is that people choose the role they want to play. If someone chooses a part then falls asleep or wanders off, we work around that. What you have to do when you think of casting a story is throw out all your pre-conceived ideas about what an 'enactment' should look like. The beauty of role play is that we can be anything we want, so don't limit people's options. The person in a wheelchair can play a winged messenger as well as the next person. This is not a performance – it is an experience. As the facilitator you are looking at what someone can get out of playing a role, not what it looks like or its dramatic effect.

When I first begin with a new group I tend to choose a story that doesn't have that many major parts so that, depending on the group, myself and my assistant can act it out. This can work quite well and people say that they enjoy watching so they are happy to come back to another session.

Then I may use a story that has a lot characters that are vital to the story but are unnamed, for example a group of villagers. I'll ask people if they would like to play one of the villagers. Often people say, 'yes, as long as I don't have to do anything', at which point I assure them that of course they don't have to do anything. So people are starting to get the idea of opting for a role and it's usually not long before they are growing in confidence.

Sometimes a person may want to play a major role of a goddess or a hero but is shy of asking – the person doesn't want to appear pushy or arrogant. One indication of this is when the person looks excited when you ask them if they want to play the part but then declines. It's always worth asking again just to make sure or trying to think of a way of making it easier for this person to accept.

Another way to involve people is to use the power of contact and relationship. A part may be a lot more attractive if it involves playing with someone you like, that could be one of the group or the staff member who is helping you.

The stabiliser

The stabiliser comes at the end of a session and may only take a few minutes but it is very important. The stabiliser is the full stop at the end of a session. Just as the warm-up or limber leads people gently into the group, so the stabiliser leads them gently out. Some groups need more of a stabiliser than others. If a group has a high level of excitement and stimulation you may want to spend a little bit longer on the stabiliser.

The aims of the stabiliser are as follows:

- it grounds the person in the here and now in preparation for going on to another setting or activity. This is important because you have been working imaginatively

- it acts as the 'full stop' or finishing part of the session; it is an essential part of the format which 'contains' the activity, thus increasing a sense of security

- it gives people a chance to separate from one another – you have been working to provide opportunities for contact and closeness.

The stabiliser may involve going around everyone in the group and thanking them for their contribution, whatever that may be (remember that people sitting watching are also contributing and need to be appreciated). It may be playing music and having a little dance and escorting people out. In one session we took a length of coloured ribbon that had been used as an object in the bridge and featured in the story and everyone held it. We then cut individual lengths for people which they were able to take away with them. This was a very satisfying way of demonstrating our membership of the group and the reality of our separateness as individuals.

I hope this information proves useful. The next step is to start trying out parts or all of a session with a group. Some people I have trained have started off just telling a story to a group and seeing what happened. Others have tried using the objects as an activity in itself and have then gradually worked it into a story session.

Below is a copy of a story I have used with a wide range of elderly groups and examples of how I adapted it accordingly, including the types of limbers, objects and stabilisers I used with it.

The Morning Star and the Evening Star

In the beginning there were only stars.

In the West dwelt Evening Star and in the East, Morning Star.

One day Morning Star decided to go and visit Evening Star, so she called her sister Little Star to her and told her: 'We are going on a journey across the sky to visit Evening Star. Pack a pouch of all the things we'll need on the journey'. So Little Star packed a pouch with all the things needed on a journey and then Morning Star and Little Star set off.

The journey was long and the night was cold so to keep up their spirits they sang and hummed together as they crossed the sky.

Now, far away on the other side of the sky, Evening Star saw their advance and decided to set obstacles in their path.

He sent the vision of a giant cactus to impede them but Little Star just reached into her pouch and pulled out a thunderbolt she had brought with her and threw it at the cactus and the vision disappeared. And on the two travelled, humming and singing as they went.

Evening Star looked out across the sky and was amazed to see Morning Star and Little Star advancing towards his house. So he decided to send another vision and this time it was of a fearsome wolf, bearing down on them slavering and howling. But Little Star just reached into her pouch and pulled out a thunderbolt, threw it at the wolf, who immediately disappeared, and the two carried on, humming and singing as they went.

Lastly, Evening Star sent a vision of a terrible monster to menace the pair but again Little Star despatched it with her thunderbolt.

And thus Morning Star and Little Star arrived at the house of Evening Star.

The house was guarded by four stars: Black Star, Yellow Star, Red Star and White Star.

Morning Star confronted them and said: 'I have travelled the sky to get here and you shall obey my command. You the Black Star are autumn and you shall stand where the night begins. You the Yellow Star are spring and shall stand near the golden sun. You the Red Star are summer and shall stand in the direction of the sun. You the White Star are winter and you shall stand where the snow begins.

The stars obeyed the command of Morning Star and they were free to enter the house of Evening Star.

Then Evening Star welcomed Morning Star and Little Star and was most gracious.

Evening Star gave his power to Morning Star and Morning Star gave her power to Evening Star and the act of creation was ready to begin.

Evening Star handed a pebble to Morning Star, who dropped it into the ocean far below and out from the ocean rose the earth.

Morning Star gave some seeds to Evening Star, who sprinkled them over the earth and immediately trees and flowers and all manner of greenery sprang up.

Then all the stars in the sky looked down from above on the earth and they smiled because they saw that what had been created was very fine.

Themes in the story

This is a creation myth from a Native American tradition. It involves the mysterious movement of the stars and the beginning of time before the creation of the earth. There are themes of coming together and that in sharing our power with one another we can create something wonderful. In a way this is a symbol of a positive group experience. There is the theme of creating something special out of very small and seemingly mundane things, the pebble and the seeds. There are familiar themes of an arduous journey and the overcoming of obstacles. There is kinship and friendship, a sense of hope and potential.

Every time I've used it, it has been enthusiastically received. It has stimulated much discussion and interest and people have been keen to take named parts such as Morning Star and Evening Star.

Sample session report from a session with a youthful elderly group

BACKGROUND

This is a very established group who have worked with a variety of stories. They are a very active and verbal group. Several members have some mobility problems but all are keen to take part and contribute. The greatest challenge is to make sure people don't talk over one another. They can occasionally be disparaging towards each other. I make it really clear this is not acceptable and encourage people to support and appreciate each other.

LIMBER OR WARM-UP

This involved an exercise familiar to the group which they enjoy. Here each person takes it in turn to lead the group in a movement which everyone else copies. All begin seated but occasionally someone does a movement that involves standing. I emphasise that we all do as much or as little as we can.

THE BRIDGE – THE OBJECTS

The objects included a toy 'microphone', which is a plastic echo chamber that slightly amplifies sound. They absolutely loved it. Everyone spoke into it and there was much laughter at the sounds they could produce. Several people sang a song into it and were cheered afterwards. I introduced the microphone saying that there was a journey in the story in which the characters sang and hummed to keep their spirits up. A woman broke into a couple of verses of 'Pack up your troubles in your old kit bag' which was wonderful and very appropriate. I hadn't connected this aspect of the story with people's experiences during the war which often involved singing together.

I also brought three pieces of brightly coloured fabric which I had purchased from an Indian sari shop. I said that the story was about stars and these were the brightest bits of material I could find. We discussed what they were made of and many people tried them on round their shoulders (one man wrapped his round his head turban style!) and looked really glamorous.

THE MAIN EVENT – THE STORY

I told the story in the version detailed above and people opted to play parts immediately. Dolly, who is in a wheelchair, said she fancied playing Morning Star but she was worried about making the journey. I said Morning Star is assisted and accompanied by her sister, Little Star, and Kitty offered to play that part and said she would help Dolly, who looked visibly relieved. When people offered to play the four guardian stars we had a brief discussion about the seasons and people's preferences and why. Everyone ended up playing the star that represented their favourite season. Monty wanted to play the monster and when no one else opted to play the wolf or the giant cactus he offered to play those too. When we had everyone organised, I asked Evening Star where in the room her house was and the guardian stars grouped themselves around her. Morning Star and Little Star set themselves up opposite her and we were ready to begin. As usual, I narrated the story as the group enacted it, but I hardly had to prompt at all. Everyone seemed really to remember the sequence of events.

THE STABILISER

The stabiliser involved people taking off their costumes and me thanking everyone for taking part. We then had a couple of verses of 'Pack up your troubles', which had been one of the songs sung into the microphone earlier. I put on some taped music and everyone left.

Sample session plan for a frail elderly group with dementia

BACKGROUND

This was a very established group and all who participated in the session on this occasion were regulars to the group. Pat came along in an agitated state, her speech, although non-verbal, was very vehement and she frequently pointed at other group members as they entered the room. She came in with Alison (my co-leader), who stayed with her and averted any altercations with a great deal of diplomacy. Pat is extremely talented with an innate dramatic sense. She is a very valued member of the group and gets a lot out of coming.

LIMBER OR WARM-UP

We used the physical limber which we always use with this group which involves passing around an inflatable ball. This produces a lot of shrieks of laughter and people really stretch and stoop to catch and throw and make decisions about who to pass the ball to. Doris, who is another long-standing member, is very quiet and withdrawn today. She is sitting with her arms tightly crossed and refuses any time she is asked if she wants the ball. I ask her if she would like to look at the ball, which is brightly coloured, or hold it for a moment, but she says no.

THE BRIDGE – THE OBJECTS

I use the microphone while Alison takes around a mask in the shape of a half moon for people to look at and try on. Most people have no idea how to use the microphone until I begin a very simple dialogue with them along the lines of 'Hello, Maisie, how are you?' and switch the mike back and forth between us until people hear themselves. Pat takes it and makes tooting noises which we both really enjoy.

THE MAIN EVENT – THE STORY

I don't use the story in its entirety. I simplify and shorten it slightly by omitting the part about the four guardian stars.

I tell the story while tea arrives and after it's gone we go around asking people what role they want to play. Pat opts to play Morning Star with Alison as Little Star. Bob tries to get Michael, his friend, to play Evening Star but when he won't he takes the part himself. I play the visions he sends to thwart Morning Star. Lily, who is in a wheelchair, plays the earth and Nora, who loves gardening, plays the seeds. Everyone else agree to play stars.

Pat plays her part with gusto. She and Alison hum as they journey across the sky. She glares at me when I come to her as one of the frightening visions sent by Evening Star and pushes me gently back across the circle and pats me on the head. After the third attempt to repulse her I inform Evening Star, 'Sir, Morning Star and Little Star have come to your house'. Bob replies, 'well then we must make them very welcome'.

THE STABILISER

In the stabiliser we thank all the stars. I become aware of the double meaning of stars in the sky and stars as celebrities. We put on music and have a dance. We dance and escort people back to the day room.

3

Stories that Contain
a Central Elderly Figure

As I planned my early sessions with elderly groups I searched for stories that contained elderly figures with whom they could identify and this is what I discovered.

Very often the elderly figure in a story is a peripheral one. They may be crucial to the development of the story: the mysterious old man who appears to give advice to the young hero, the kindly old woman who shelters the heroine. But they are not usually the central figure.

As in stories so in life, where elderly people are often marginalised and inconspicuous.

Doris Lessing's wonderful book *The Diary of Jane Somers*[1] describes a relationship between a woman and her elderly neighbour. The reality of elderly person's lives had hardly impinged on Jane's consciousness until that time. She had scarcely noticed elderly people existed. Through the relationship, her eyes are opened to a whole section of the population who had previously been invisible.

This is one of the reasons I really like to use stories that feature an elderly person in a much more conspicuous role.

The portrayal does not have to be flattering, as in the African story of 'The old woman and the tree children'. I think this is important: the stereotype of the sweet old lady is probably just as restricting as the stereotype of the malicious crone.

In fairy stories the elderly person is often an evil crone or malicious old man who wants to do harm to the hero or heroine, who are usually young.

1   Doris Lessing (1985) *The Diary of Jane Somers*. London: Penguin.

Fairy stories tend to present characters in a very flat, one-dimensional light and then polarise them. Thus one person is all good while another is all bad. It is not necessarily that fairy stories are exclusively for children. Originally they were popular with all ages. They do, however, deal psychologically with early stages of personality development and hence are attractive to children because they are dealing with issues with which a child can identify. As Bettleheim writes in *The Uses of Enchantment*: 'fairy tales are so meaningful to children in helping them cope with the psychological problems of growing up and integrating their personalities'[2].

Very often, the story focuses on a character who is very young and pits them against the 'grown ups'. These grown ups are often not their parents' age – psychologically this would make it very frightening to the child because it would be being asked to enter into competition with the parent and in some cases defeat the parent. Powerful old people make good adversaries which the child can fantasise about defeating without arousing uncomfortable feelings, especially if these old people are presented as malevolent!

Obviously, these stories are not aiming to give an accurate portrayal of elderly people. However, unfortunately, a lot of children don't have any other contact with elderly people to balance what is often a negative representation in fairy stories.

This is not to say that I never use fairy tales – included here is the Grimm's story of 'The three dancing princesses' but this story is unusual in that it has an elderly man as the 'hero'.

We may come across stories that show elderly people and the ageing process in general in a positive light. This would be the story that portrays the older person as the person with wisdom and life experience. The community is benefited and enriched by having such a person in its midst.

In the Yugoslavian tale of the villagers buying wisdom (see Chapter 5) I often say that the village is full of young people and for some reason not a lot of old people live there. I ask groups where they think you can get wisdom and a common reply is that you acquire it through life experience – it is not something you can get from a book, you have to live it. In doing this I am going some small way to helping to redress the widely held cultural and

2   Bruno Bettleheim (1975) *The Uses of Enchantment*, Penguin, London, p.14.

social prejudices against older people, especially the stereotype of the 'doddery old fool'.

Two of the stories I have included in this section contain a central character, in both cases an old woman, who lives alone and is independent. In the Russian tale, Babka is very much part of her rural community. She has her own home but is surrounded by neighbours. She is not alone. The first thing she does when she hears the plans of the courtiers is to run and tell her neighbours and the story ends with her celebrating with them. The woman in another story, Yaaba, is very much more isolated but the story ends with her acceptance into the life of the village while maintaining her independence. For many older people in residential homes or nursing homes this would be a very attractive prospect: the best of both worlds – to have one's independence but to know that people are around if you need them.

Yaaba

Once there was a village where lived a man and his wife and their baby child. On the outskirts of the village at the place where all the villagers went to draw water lived an old woman called Yaaba. Yaaba lived on her own in her little hut and never did any harm to anyone. However, the people in the village called her a witch. They encouraged their children to throw stones at her and call her names when she went to draw water, and if any mishap befell a person they invariably blamed it on Yaaba.

One day the man's young child became ill with a fever and no one in the village could cure him. The man's wife came from another village and she didn't believe the things that were said about Yaaba. On the contrary, she thought the old woman had great wisdom. In her desperation and while her husband was working in the fields, she stole out of the village with the child under her robe. Yaaba received the woman courteously and took one look at the child and began to grind herbs into a paste and lay them on the child's forehead. The women sat together with the baby and very soon the fever lessened and his mother took him home overjoyed. Mindful of her husband's displeasure she did not tell anyone of her visit to Yaaba, not even the child who grew into a fine, strong boy.

However, the boy did not like to taunt and tease Yaaba the way his friends did and as he got older he began to make a point of talking to the old woman whenever he had to fetch water for his mother.

In time the two became friends and the boy would often visit Yaaba at her hut, being careful not to let his father or the other villagers know.

A time came when there was drought in the land and people pointed the finger at Yaaba and muttered beneath their breath and hoarded their water jealously. In the boy's household they had one pot of precious water left and every day they scanned the horizon anxiously for any sign of cloud or rain.

The boy realised it was days since he had seen Yaaba and at the first opportunity he slipped away and hurried to her hut.

There he found her lying sick on her bed. Her hut was a mess and she had nothing to drink. 'Don't worry, Yaaba,' said the boy, 'I am going to take care of you.'

With that he hurried home and took food and what little water they had left and quickly returned to Yaaba.

There he set about helping her drink and eat, cleaned her hut and made her more comfortable.

Meanwhile the boy's father had returned home and discovered the water had gone. He enquired in the village and someone told him that he had seen his son taking it to the home of Yaaba. He was furious and it didn't take much for a whole crowd of villagers to join with him in a plan to burn down Yaaba's hut.

Armed with sticks they were making their way out of the village when they came across the boy who was on his way home.

His father took him roughly by the shoulders and demanded: 'What are you doing going to the hut of that witch and taking our water? Answer me before I give you a beating!'.

With that he lifted up his stick to beat the boy but at that moment his wife ran out from the crowd and grabbed his arm.

'Stop!' she said, 'Enough of this madness; if it wasn't for the woman you call witch you wouldn't have a son. She was the one who broke his fever that time when he was tiny. You owe her a debt of gratitude'.

The man hesitated for a moment while the village waited to see what would happen.

Suddenly someone shouted and pointed skyward and looking up they saw huge, black clouds looming overhead and before they knew it fat drops of rain were landing on their upturned faces.

There was much excitement as people ran indoors to get pots to catch the first of the rain. Yaaba was momentarily forgotten.

The drought was over but a subtle difference came in the villagers' attitude towards the old woman. The boy and his mother went openly to care for her and the husband did not complain.

They even asked Yaaba if she wanted to move her hut so it was closer to the other villagers but she said she was happy where she was and people could come and visit her.

Never again did the villagers taunt Yaaba.

Themes in the story

'Yaaba' turned out to be a good story to use with groups who are new to each other and this way of working. It is a simple tale without any magical elements and with lots for elderly people to identify with.

The background to the story is quite interesting. One of my first elderly groups was in St Pancras hospital and one of the original members was a woman called Ann. Right from the beginning, Ann seemed to have an affinity with, and insight into, stories, and she listened avidly to every story, sometimes getting quite irritable at Michael, another regular in the group who loved to talk and flirt.

One week I used a story from the North American tradition which was set in an eternal winter among blizzards and ice.

At the end of the session Ann called me over to speak to her and made an unusual request: 'next time let's have a hot story, maybe one set in a desert or something'. I was so pleased at her initiative that I promised I would – only to have to wrack my brains for a suitable one.

What I ended up doing was adapting the story of an African film I had seen where the central character was an old woman called Yaaba and there was a friendship with a young boy. I really couldn't remember much more than that so had to make up elements of my own.

However, I was able to go back the next week with this story and Ann remembered my promise. She was really delighted and I made a point of telling the group that the idea for the story had come from her. She was a very sophisticated and clever woman who found living with the effects of her stroke very hard and would sometimes become very depressed. I remember turning up for the session to find that she had suffered a stroke to the other side of her body, so had lost even more of her abilities. Very often it is unknown how long a person will be afflicted and Ann did recover a little but she died soon afterwards. I still remember her clearly and with great fondness.

The old lady in the story is a positive figure but one who is not appreciated by the people in her community. Worse, she is the object of scorn and derision and in some cases violence. Sad to say this is a common experience for a lot of elderly people, and certainly when I have told this story I have heard a lot of people identify with it. A woman told me she had had stones thrown at her by children who called her rude names.

A motif in the story is the relationship of the very old to the very young and how this can often be a mutually satisfying one. It is less and less common these days when there is so little connection between generations. I myself grew up without grandparents on either side of the family and had very little contact with old people until I came to work with them as a drama therapist. For me there have been a number of people over the years who have been like grandparents to me and with whom I feel a very special bond.

The old lady in the story is independent and she retains her independence even after being invited into the life of the village. I have heard many old people say that they did not want to go and live with their daughter and son because they 'liked their own space', even when they were finding it difficult to manage on their own.

This story speaks to anyone who has felt misunderstood and unappreciated. It is really unfair that someone who heals and helps should be accused of being a witch but it is a common enough scenario.

Using the story in a session

In the session it was only fair that Ann play Yaaba, which she did with tremendous dignity. I had a volunteer who helped with the group who was a great favourite of Ann's. His name was Bill. Ann and he had a rapport and she often opted to play roles alongside him. Ann wanted him to play the young boy which was delightful. Bill was at least fifty and often very short of breath but he somehow managed to capture the youthfulness of the role. It was very touching to see the two interacting in the story, for in 'real life' Bill was a bit gruff and Ann was quite reserved. It was another example of a role giving an opportunity for people to express a part of their contemporary relationship that they wouldn't normally, within the context of a story.

Babka and the Golden Bird

There was once an old woman who lived by herself in a village on the edge of a magnificent forest. Her name was Babka.

Although she was poor she considered herself very fortunate. She had just enough to eat from the money she earned collecting sticks in the forest and selling them in her village and the couple of chickens that kept her supplied with eggs. She had many friends but most of all she was surrounded by all manner of wild creatures and, best of all, birds.

In the winter life was hard for the people on the edge of the forest. The cold was cruel and ice formed on the tops of windows and snow sloped over the edge of cottage roofs. Babka pitied the poor birds who came to her garden to drink from the pond only to find it frozen over. From her small store of bread she would scatter crumbs and the little birds would come at her call and sometimes perch on her hand and fix her with their small, bright eyes.

One day Babka was in the forest gathering wood when she heard the sound of horses' hooves. She quickly hid behind a tree and watched as two horsemen cantered into the clearing and dismounted. They were dressed very finely in the uniforms of the king and they appeared to be surveying the land.

Babka overhead their conversation and her heart sank. 'This would indeed be an ideal location for a winter palace. If this forest was cleared there would be more than enough acreage and the peasants could move their village to the other side of the mountain.' The two nodded in agreement, mounted their horses and rode off. Poor Babka hurried home, 'clear the forest, move the village', the idea was unthinkable. But Babka knew that the wealthy usually got what they wanted. When she got to the village she told the bad news of what she'd heard to her neighbours and they were equally dismayed 'What can we do?' they said, 'we are poor people and the king is rich and powerful!'

Babka left them and with a heavy heart hurried home.

As soon as she got home she put a pot on the fire and went out to feed the birds. But what did she find at the bottom of her garden, under a bush and only half alive, but a little wounded bird? Its feathers were dull and brown and its eyes clouded, but it let Babka take it in her hands where she could feel the tremulous beat of its tiny heart. She took it into her cottage and kept it warm by the fire. She spooned a little broth into its beak and tore up crumbs of bread and left them by its head. Then, worn out, she sat down beside the fire and fell asleep.

When she awoke the room was illuminated by a golden glow. Turning, she saw to her astonishment that the bird had recovered and stood before her, glorious and bright. Its tail feathers were a brilliant burnished copper and its back glowed like the sun. She was even more astonished when it spoke to her and said, 'Babka, you are a good and kind woman. I am going to give you three wishes, not just for your kindness towards me but for all the many kindnesses you have shown the forest creatures over the years. What is it that you wish?'.

Babka thought for a moment then replied, 'There are men who want to destroy the forest. I wish that they would go away and choose another place to build their palace'.

'Granted,' said the bird.

'And I wish that the brook in my garden did not freeze over in the wintertime so the birds always had water to drink.'

'Granted,' said the bird, 'but Babka, wish something for yourself with your last wish.'

'Alright,' said Babka, 'I wish that I had a fire that never went out so that I didn't have to gather wood for it every day.'

'Granted,' said the bird.

Suddenly Babka heard a clamouring in her garden and, looking out, she saw birds fluttering around the brook that had been frozen solid. It now had steam rising from it and was flowing freely.

She turned back to find the golden bird had disappeared. The fire in her grate was glowing brightly where before it had almost died down.

Suddenly there was a knock at the door and opening it there stood the two courtiers, who asked her for water and a seat by the fire to warm themselves.

Babka fetched them water and what little food she could spare while they talked. She overheard them saying, 'On second thoughts this region is not such an ideal spot. I think perhaps we should travel on across the mountains to find the location for the king's winter palace'. They thanked her for her hospitality and left.

Babka excitedly went to share the good news with her neighbours.

Themes in the story

The major theme in the story, and one I come back to again and again, is the theme of an unassuming person's worth being recognised and rewarded. Babka quietly goes about her business and a simple act of kindness transforms her life. Her act is characteristic of her lack of selfishness – the bird has to urge her to use at least one of her wishes for herself. Interestingly, what she wishes does not change her life in any major way – her life will carry on largely as it did before. She is, in a very positive sense, easily satisfied. This is significant and is in stark contrast to many stories such as the story of the old woman who lived in a vinegar bottle. Here the old woman is portrayed as being very bitter and complaining. A passing fairy takes pity on her and gives her a little cottage to live in but shortly afterwards the old woman is grumbling again. The fairy transforms her into a duchess and then a queen and then an empress, but the old woman is insatiable – nothing will ever satisfy her. Eventually her life comes full circle and she is back to living in the vinegar bottle.

This woman has a great inner emptiness that can never be satisfied materially, although the focus of her longing may be material things. She has a spiritual poverty, unlike Babka who, although poor, considers herself fortunate.

The other figure in the story which is very important is the wounded bird. On a symbolic level it is the nondescript which, on further examination (or to the eyes of those who see through these things), reveals great beauty and value. This is a recurring theme in stories, appearing as the apple with jewels inside among other things. It is a powerful symbol in work with most groups of people, but particularly those who are disadvantaged or underestimated, because what it presents is a character who sees beneath the appearance of things to the inner beauty.

Babka's relationship with the bird is one of mutual healing. This is important – we can forget how good it is to give as well as to receive. Many people in residential care are in the position of receiving help and healing but are denied the opportunity to offer it. Stories such as these provide an opportunity. This doesn't have to be limited to the person playing the role. Often I ask the group, 'What would you do with a little bird that is wounded?'.

Using the story in a session

In a group where most people had had strokes there was a lot of mental agility but difficulty in speaking. I would know from someone's face lighting up that they had something to say in answer to a question I had asked. Then the task would be to give that person my attention for the time it took to understand the answer. With this story I once asked people, 'If you were a forest animal what would you be?'. In this case of people who had difficulty speaking I provided examples. I didn't name the animals but asked people to choose from a range of possibilities, such as a large animal or a small one, a fierce animal or a shy one. The process is one of elimination and goes some way to preserving the integrity of the person's choice. A regular participant in our sessions was Ossie, who had been a sea captain. He had difficulty remembering names and there was often quite a long gap between asking a question and receiving an answer. This was a symptom of the stroke he had suffered and sometimes it was difficult to know if he had heard or not. On this occasion I asked him, 'If you were a forest creature what would you be?'. I asked him if he wanted to be a fierce creature and he replied, 'No, I have spent too much of my life being fierce. I want to be gentle'. He said this very regretfully and wept a little. He eventually chose to be a deer.

A lot of people in the group had Russian ancestry; some had come to England at the end of the last war. Often they had come from very rural places and the world described in the story of Babka was not too far removed from the Russia of their childhoods. They seemed really to enjoy talking about it and I was fascinated to hear about this very different world.

People in the group really sympathised with Babka's predicament and how vulnerable she was in the path of faceless bureaucracy.

Sometimes your choice of prop influences your choice of story rather than the other way around. On this occasion, my co-therapist had become the proud owner of a battery operated chicken from China. This chicken was made of tin and painted bright red and yellow. When you turned a switch on its underside it would begin to trundle along the floor and deposit little white eggs in its path. We knew of members of our groups who would be delighted by this so we were keen to incorporate it into a story. We did this by saying it was one of Babka's chickens and the group really enjoyed watching it 'perform' as part of the warm-up, but also looking more closely at it, seeing what it was made of and how it worked.

With another group I asked people what they would wish if they had three wishes. I was shocked at the response. So many people wished to be young again or to have good health. One woman wished to go home and looked tearful as she said it. It made me realise what powerful things wishes are and asking people to name their wishes arouses some very deep feelings.

Granny Evergreen

Once there were two children, a boy and a girl, who lived on the edge of the wood with their mother.

One day she became ill and, having a pining for strawberries, she sent them out to gather them in the wood. The children came upon a bush that was full of wild strawberries, sweet and red, and began to fill their basket with the soft fruit. Suddenly there appeared an old woman dressed entirely in green who introduced herself as Granny Evergreen. She asked them what they had in the basket and they replied, 'Strawberries, grandmother, for our mother who is sick'. Granny Evergreen replied, 'Oh, children, I would love some wild strawberries but am too old and stiff to gather them for myself. Please give me the strawberries you have in your basket'. The children knew their mother was waiting at home for the fruit but they gave their strawberries to the old woman and began to pick some more. A moment later, Granny Evergreen returned and gave them back their fruit and in addition two flowers, one white and one blue, with this instruction: 'Take these flowers and water them daily and never ever sleep on a quarrel'.

The children thanked the old woman and returned home. They gave the strawberries to their mother, who recovered almost as soon as she tasted them and placed the flowers in water where they bloomed continuously.

However, one evening they quarrelled and ignored their mother's request that they make up and not sleep with anger.

The next day they rose to see their pretty flowers blackened and fading, and they did not return to their white and blue colouring until the children had shed many tears on them. From then on they took great care never to sleep with anger and Granny Evergreen's flowers bloomed once more.

Themes in the story

There is a moral to the story about not sleeping with anger. It recognises the reality of conflict in relationships but advises sorting things out sooner rather than later lest things begin to 'fester', as did the flowers in the story.

It portrays the children being rewarded by their kindness to the old lady. She makes a request of them and their willingness to respond is what is rewarded.

The story also has a very simple narrative structure, so I have used it many times with new groups or groups whose concentration is short or who get confused easily.

The Old Woman and the Tree Children

There was an old woman who was all alone. She had to work to feed and support herself and life was very hard. She had no children to care for her in her later years and her bones were weary.

One day she went into the forest to gather kindling to sell to make a little money to buy food. She went deep into the forest and came upon a wonderful tree that she had never before noticed. The tree was blooming with huge flowers and was a sight to behold.

The old woman decided to rest a while beneath the tree to get her breath back. She settled herself down with a big sigh and was startled to hear the tree address her.

'Why do you sigh so, old woman, are you sick?' said the tree.

'I am not sick,' said the woman, 'but I have to work hard to make ends meet and I am very tired.'

'Have you no children to support you in your old age?' said the tree.

'No,' replied the old woman, 'I had children but they grew and moved away and now I am all alone.'

'I will give you some children then,' said the tree, 'but you must not beat or scold them lest you drive them away.'

At once the blossoms from the tree transformed into children. They came down chattering and laughing and the woman took them home

From then on the life of the old woman was made very much easier. Each child was responsible for its own chores and all worked diligently. There was one child that was smaller than all the rest. The bigger children said to the woman, 'This little one must not work. You must feed her when she is hungry and never scold her'.

The old woman was more than happy to agree – all her work was done for her and all she had to do was to feed the littlest child when she cried for food.

This carried on for some time in perfect harmony until one day the little child asked for food and the old woman berated her saying, 'Get it yourself you lazy brat, have I not enough to do without running around after you?'.

The little girl cried and cried because she had been so rudely scolded. When the older children returned they wanted to know why she was so distressed.

When they found out they went to the old woman and they said, 'You have broken the agreement you made with our mother the tree, and so we must leave you and return to her'.

The old woman pleaded with them not to leave but they were adamant. They returned to the forest and once again adorned the tree with blossom. The old woman spent the rest of her days alone.

Themes in the story

This is a very interesting story and appeals a lot to elderly groups despite its downbeat ending.

The issue of the old woman's isolation is incredibly relevant today, possibly more than ever. When I train staff who work in residential homes they tell me their experience is that the elderly person has little or no contact with family members. This may not be true everywhere. Certainly some residential homes make a concerted effort to involve people's families in their care, which implies that the contact with the family is there to maintain.

Many of the care workers I trained were from other cultures and they exclaimed over what they saw as the English disregard for their elderly relatives.

The old woman's predicament is not to be underestimated – in many cultures a good reason for raising children was the expectation of their support in old age.

It is also very clear that the children were there to work and this is very common in lots of cultures, particularly Africa which is where this story comes from.

Using the story in a session

On one occasion I asked a group what they thought should happen to the old woman once she had broken the agreement and scolded the littlest child. Some people suggested far harsher penalties than the loss of the children! One woman said, 'it's very true, when you first have something good you really appreciate it but after a time it's really easy to start taking it for granted until you lose it'.

The group was run by myself and another drama therapist and was in a long-stay hospital. It was made up of very frail elderly people in wheelchairs. Most people had had strokes. There was one lady who was mobile who was very good friends with another lady in a chair. Both were enthusiastic members of the group, which was very established.

People lived in wards of about six people, so meeting up with others from the other wards was often a treat. We realised that and allowed time at the beginning of the group for people to re-establish contact with one another. One of us would stay in the room to do this while the other went to get people. This could involve pointing out other people in the group, assisting someone waving at another group member and asking people who they would like to sit beside. It meant that by the time we had everyone and we were ready to start there was conversation and excitement in the room.

We incorporated the objects into the warm-up as we had a couple of African drums. These were very beautiful, well-crafted instruments. Some people were quick to bang the drums while others seemed to like the feel of the skin. We assisted people, in some cases holding the drum at an angle so that, for example, one man who had use of one arm that was immensely strong could give it a resounding thwack!

One woman in the group had a song she always loved to sing which was called 'Rowan tree'. She needed very little encouragement to sing the song while others drummed along, and this provided the cue for others to have a go and sing accompanied. We said it was a perfect choice of song as there was a tree in the story.

The other prop we brought to this particular session was a piece of tie-dyed fabric from the Gambia. The colours were very strong; in fact they had a tendency to come off on people's hands, from which we realised that the dye had not been fixed. We asked if anyone had any ideas on how to fix dye in fabric and received a number of really good suggestions. A woman encouraged us to try and wear the fabric as a turban and then Alfred wanted to try it as a turban, which really made us all laugh as he looked very serious. Doris, who had an excellent memory and love for old movies, said he looked just like Dorothy Lamour in 'Road to Rio'.

We then told the story. Usually this meant one of us told the story while the other sat beside whoever was hard of hearing to make sure they could hear as much as possible. The group sat in a semi-circle because of the number of wheelchairs, so the storyteller would move around the semi-circle while she told the story.

Because this was a very established group we tended to leave all the parts open just to see what people wanted to do.

Immediately we asked for volunteers, Christina, who was very mobile, offered to play the 'poor old woman'. This made the rest of the casting straightforward because as soon as we asked for people to play her children her best friend Agnes offered – I asked her if she wanted to play an older child or the littlest one who needs feeding and doesn't like being scolded. She immediately opted to play the littlest child.

We then needed someone to play the tree. At this point Eva, a nurse, entered the group. She was a particular favourite of Martha, who was very shy. I asked Eva if she would be one of the children of the tree and she said yes. I then asked if anyone would like to play the tree who is like the mother of all the little children. I think because it involved having contact with Eva, Martha agreed to play the tree. Another woman also wanted to play the tree, so we helped the two sit beside each other.

When the enactment began Christina played her part beautifully. She was a lady who could be immensely charming to people she liked but she and Martha didn't usually get on so it was quite a surprise to us when Martha in her role as the tree reached out to comfort Christina when she told her she was all alone in the world.

Christina looked delighted when the 'children' emerged from the tree and we had great fun asking her what work she wanted us to do for her – she had us scurrying around all over the place. We saw how delighted people looked at the spectacle of us running around doing chores, so we went out to other members of the group and asked them what we could do for them.

Christina loved her 'littlest child' and I could see it was going to be difficult for her to scold her as per the story. However, Agnes started playing the child as quite a cheeky little thing and very soon Christina lost patience with her and scolded her. She was not keen on the idea of not feeding her, but she did chide her.

The loss of the children was very powerful as both Agnes and Eva played it quite regretfully as if they didn't really want to go.

The creativity in the group really showed itself at the end when the old woman is left alone as a man suggested, 'go and find the tree'.

Christina did so and we redesigned the ending without, I think, compromising it in any way. We said that every day the old woman would go and sit beside the tree and enjoy the sight and smell of the blossoms and remember her children.

We finished the session with appreciation for everyone's contribution and hand dancing.

The Three Blue Hats

There once was a boatman called Simon who needed wood to patch up the hull of his boat. One cold, wintry day he went out on to the moors to look for wood and failed to notice a mist descending. Before he knew it he was thoroughly lost.

Now he felt fear plucking at his coat tails, for night was falling and it wouldn't do to be caught out on the moors in the freezing cold. He stumbled on, desperately trying to find his bearings when all at once he saw a light in the distance.

With the determination of a drowning man Simon pushed on towards the light until he came within sight of a little crofter's cottage. He was so grateful to see a candle shining in the window and there was a tradition of hospitality in these parts so he had no fear of being turned away. He knocked loudly on the door and called out 'let me in!'.

There was a scuffling sound from inside the cottage and the door was opened just enough for someone to peer out. The young man quickly explained, 'I'm lost on the moor and freezing with cold, could you let me in to share your fire till morning?'.

The person seemed to confer with others in the room and then slowly pulled back the door. Simon quickly entered and what should he see sitting in front of a big roaring fire but three old ladies. Not a word was said but one motioned to Simon a place by the hearth and he lay down, pulling his great coat around him. Simon was greatly intrigued by the strangeness of the women so he made a big thing out of pretending to be asleep but all the time he kept one eye open. Time passed and when the old women were satisfied Simon was asleep they looked each at each other and started to laugh. Then one of them went to the dresser and pulled out a blue cap which she put on.

'Bishop of Carlisle, Bishop of Carlisle, Bishop of Carlisle,' she chanted and promptly disappeared. Simon, feigning sleep on the hearth, nearly gave himself away with surprise. He managed to recover his composure as the second and then the third old woman went to the dresser, put on a blue cap, chanted 'Bishop of Carlisle, Bishop of Carlisle, Bishop of Carlisle' and then disappeared. Simon rose and looked around the room and when he had satisfied himself that the cottage was empty save for himself, he too went to the dresser and found a blue cap. His curiosity was so great that he could not resist. He put on the cap, chanted 'Bishop of Carlisle, Bishop of Carlisle, Bishop of Carlisle' and found himself whirling through the air at a great speed. Before he could catch his breath he came to earth with a thud. For a moment he had no idea where he was. He was on a stone floor in a very large, dark room. As his sight adjusted he saw huge barrels all around him and he heard the echoing sound of giggles coming from not very far away. He was in some kind of wine cellar and, looking behind a neighbouring cask, he saw the three old women lying on the floor getting very drunk with bottles in their hands.

Suddenly there was the sound of keys grating in locks. The old women looked startled and in unison chanted 'Stokey moor' three times and disappeared.

Simon hardly had time to think before he was hoisted to his feet by a burly guard and found himself face to face with the constable who said, 'aha, so we caught you, you rascal, and surrounded by evidence!'. He pointed to the bottles left lying on the floor by the three old women's hasty departure. 'We've been lying in wait for you these past three nights. You're going to rue the day you dared to steal from the Bishop's wine cellar!'.

Poor Simon was brought before a court headed by the Bishop whose cellar it was.

One of the guards roughly pulled off his cap saying, 'show some respect to a man of the cloth'.

He was found guilty of stealing and sentenced to be burnt at the stake!

What could Simon do? His hands were bound and he was surrounded by hundreds of the Bishop's men.

Before long he was tied to a stake and burning faggots were placed about his feet. The Bishop asked him, 'do you have any last requests?'.

Suddenly Simon remembered his cap. 'I would like to die with my hat on like a true gentleman,' he said.

A guard placed his hat on his head and without hesitation he chanted 'Stokey moor' three times. All at once he was rushing through the air and he landed with a bump and found himself out on the moor. His hands were still tied to the stake and he looked and saw that it was a fine piece of wood that would do a really good job of repairing his hull.

Laughing, he made his way home with a really good story to tell all his friends.

Themes in the story

I really like this story and have had great fun doing it with groups. It does involve three witch-type characters getting very drunk but I have never encountered anyone in a group feeling demeaned by this; in fact people have really giggled at it. It is a Northumbrian or border country story.

Using the story in a session

What made this story memorable was the involvement of Dot, who took the part of one of the old women. It was her first and last role play in the sessions, and I sometimes use it as an example of the length of time it can take to build up trust and that relationships may develop in very small ways over what may be long periods of time. I shall never forget meeting Dot. I had seen her several times before. She was in a chair with wheels that she could move around wards and corridors. She was very tiny with a very wrinkled, brown face. I had heard that she had lived on the streets for years and she spent her time wandering the hospital. This particular morning I was feeling very cheerful. I called out 'morning, Dot!', to which she yelled really loudly, 'f... off!'.

A regular member of our group shared a room with Dot so I would often ask her if she wanted to join us and she would always refuse. I often asked because I wanted to keep the invitation open.

After several years, we came into the day room to set up for the session and Dot was there. As we started to bring people in and the music came on, Dot withdrew to a corner of the room. I asked her if she was alright where she was and she said yes. During the session we made various attempts to involve her but to no avail. Soon it became quite common for Dot to stay in the day room while we ran the session; we would continue to maintain contact and in between times I would stop and have a chat to her when I saw her in the corridor. We discovered I lived in the same part of East London that she had lived as a child. I said I had cats and she told me she had had seven, which she had had to feed herself on 'a shilling a week'.

A breakthrough came in one session when I went over to show Dot one of the props. It was a cream and white shell that was just big enough to fit into the palm of my hand. I knew her eyesight was very poor, so I approached her very gently saying, 'would like to have a look at this, Dot?'.

Dot peered down at the shell and shrieked 'what is it?'.

I explained it was a shell.

Dot looked visibly relieved. 'I thought it was a little animal,' she said. She took the shell in her hand. 'Oh, it's heavy isn't it?'. She seemed really to enjoy feeling and touching it.

From then on it was the part of the session she would always take part in; even if it meant sitting in another part of the room for the rest of the time, she would draw herself closer when we told her we had brought some things to show her. Obviously we always asked her if she wanted to play such and such a role and she always declined in her own inimicable style. However, on this occasion when I asked her if she wanted to play one of the three magical old woman she said, 'Alright', which just goes to show that you can never tell how a person will respond even when you think you know them really well!

We had brought in a whole selection of hats for the warm-up and we spent a lot of time helping people to try them on and model them and exclaim over how wonderful they looked. Hats are a great prop to use in a group because they can create a look or a character without more complicated dressing up and they're easy for people in wheelchairs both to hold and try on.

As soon as we started casting the story Glen was nominated to play the role of Simon. Glen was the activities organiser, who could sometimes be prevailed upon to join the sessions, much to the delight of the residents. He was a young man who loved music and going out to concerts. He was marvellous at his job and had a wonderful relationship with the residents.

All three 'old ladies' were sitting together at one side of the semi-circle, and Glen as Simon started the story over the other side of the room and made his way across the wintry moor towards the cottage.

When he knocked on the door (sound effects provided by exaggerated knocking sounds on a table top) one of the woman called out 'hello?'.

'Simon' explained who he was very politely and asked if he could be let in. Immediately all three women were concerned he not catch cold and had to be laughingly reminded by the narrator to be suspicious and grudgingly let him in. When a group begins to make a story their own it can be the most fun and it is up to the narrator to steer the story along loosely, incorporating the changes wherever possible and leaving plenty of room for invention on the part of the players. All three women were in wheelchairs, so it was up to the co-leader to 'whisk them away' at the point they donned their caps.

When it was Glen's turn he did a wonderful show of flying through the air, spinning around with arms flailing and landing on the floor.

The Bishop was a great part for Alfred, who always took a role. We had quite an ornate piece of cloth that I had found in an Indian sari shop in the East End of London which he wore over his shoulders. He also made a point of blessing people with his two fingers extended. Since his stroke his speech had gone, but he had the most sonorous, melodic voice which he used very expressively. His sentencing of 'Simon' to the stake was most impressive.

One of the props in the session was a piece of driftwood which people had really enjoyed looking at and touching. We used this as the stake in the story, to the amusement of the group as it was only about six inches long and not the sort of thing you could tie someone to at all.

The Pedlar of Swaffham

There was once an old pedlar who lived in a village in Swaffham surrounded by his grown children and grandchildren.

He had worked his whole life and now he was elderly he was poor as a church mouse. But he thanked heaven every night that he had his health and his wife and all his children were well and happy.

One night he had a vivid dream, so vivid that he woke his wife to tell her.

'Wake up, Elsie,' he said, 'I've just had the strangest dream. A voice telling me to travel to London Bridge and good will come of it.'

As you can imagine his wife was none to happy too be woken at such an hour.

The next night he had the same dream and the night after that. By this time his wife said to him, 'Go, John, go to London Bridge and see what the dream means'.

Everyone else in the village was amazed that John was considering such a journey, which on foot and for a young man could take three or four days.

But the following day John set off with a stout stick, a knapsack full of food prepared by his dear wife, and a bag full of trinkets and pegs and ribbons to sell on the stall.

John walked steadily and rested often. Sometimes he was accompanied by a fellow traveller, sometimes he walked alone. Sometimes the sun shone and sometimes it rained.

On John walked through the Kent countryside, and when he got tired he sustained himself by recalling his strange dream. At night he stayed at monasteries or in someone's barn and on the evening of the seventh day he came within sight of the great city of London.

What an exciting place it was, teeming with people and the air full of the cries of hawkers and the melodies of dozens of different voices.

Straight away, John asked directions for London Bridge and he found himself standing on it just as the sun was sinking in the east. John was so excited. Now, he thought, I will discover the meaning of my dream.

The next morning he returned and set up a little stall of his wares and waited expectedly.

All day he stood with people milling here and there, a great hurley burley going about their business. Occasionally someone stopped to have a look at what he was selling and he sold a few things but not much.

The day ended as it had begun and John's spirits began to droop a little.

The next day he was up at dawn and positioned on the bridge. The day passed and still nothing happened.

On the third day he began to lose faith. He had only a few coppers left to buy a room for the night and faced returning home looking not a little foolish. Suddenly he was approached by one of the shopkeepers who had a shop on one side of the bridge.

'Old man, I've been watching you these past three days and I'm curious to know what you're doing here. You don't seem to be selling much and look like you should be home in front of your own fire!'

'Well,' said John, 'I'm beginning to think the same thing. I had a dream that said "go to London Bridge, some good will come of it" and the dream was so strong that I came. But I've been standing here these past three days and nothing has happened.'

The shopkeeper burst out laughing at the old man.

'You came to London Bridge because of a dream? You can't go giving credit to dreams. I've been having dreams about treasure buried under a hawthorn tree in a pedlar's garden in Swaffham but you don't see me going haring up there to see if it's true!'

John couldn't quite believe his ears. The shopkeeper kindly invited him back to his home for a meal but John excused himself, saying he thought it was time to return home to his wife and family and with that he set off straight away.

When he came within sight of Swaffham he was foot sore and weary but he couldn't wait to check out his suspicions. His wife was overjoyed to see him and amazed when he grabbed a spade and called for his strong sons to help him and went out into the patch of ground at the back of his cottage.

There he began to dig at the old hawthorn tree. He managed to uproot it and was digging down into the earth when he heard the unmistakable sound of metal against metal. By then his sons had arrived and they helped him dig to uncover an old leather chest.

Drawing it into the light, they opened it and there were hundreds of gold coins glistening and glinting in the fading sunshine.

What a celebration they had in John's house that night! There was more than enough for John and his wife for the rest of their days and plenty to give to his sons and daughters and some left over to contribute to the village itself.

And that night John slept soundly in his bed untroubled by dreams...

Themes in the story

In the original story, John is a younger man. I wanted John to be older and have a grown up family that he was anxious to provide for, as this is something that I have heard a lot of older people talk about. In the original story it took the younger man three days to walk to London so I thought it would probably take an elderly man about seven!

I also like John being older so that we can see that it is not just young people who go off on adventures in order to follow their dreams. It may seem as if the opportunities to do so get less and less as we get older but it is never too late.

Again the story gives an image of intuitive understanding or inner knowing that is very positive. The dream arises from John's own unconscious and it proves to be accurate. The character of the London shopkeeper represents someone who receives the inner urging but refuses to act on it.

The story is a classic example of a myth in the tradition of the return journey. The story is saying that the precious thing we seek is in our own back yard but the journey is vital. It is a motif common in stories throughout the world. There is a Tibetan story of a young man who eavesdrops on a council of animals in the forest. He hears them talking about how foolish the humans are in a neighbouring village who toil across the mountain for water every day. They don't realise that under an old tree in the headman's garden is a spring of fresh water that would provide for the whole village.

We are taught to look outside of ourselves for satisfaction and then are amazed when satisfaction proves elusive. These stories communicate a deep psychological truth, which is that the treasure we seek is within. I think this is a very good message to be giving to people in the later stages of life and also people whose opportunities for asserting themselves in the world are dwindling. At any time we can look within. The symbolic nature of stories nourishes the inner life and affirms this process.

The journey is important; it is an act of faith, it is a struggle and struggle is important. What is often not recognised is how as human beings we need to exert ourselves and meet challenges – this stimulates us and increases our confidence. This need is there from the moment of conception. The struggle to be born releases a hormone which stimulates a membrane in the baby's lungs which helps it breathe. Babies born by Caesarian don't struggle in the same way and this process is missed and consequently they are often smaller and weaker than babies born normally. The opportunities to meet challenges and overcome obstacles may decrease as we get older. People work to make life as easy as possible for the older person without realising that an easy life is not necessarily a happy or satisfying one.

In the theme of the importance of following your dreams, the story has similarities with 'The Bird of Happiness' and 'How the Villagers Found Wisdom' (see Chapter 5).

There are many similarities between stories and dreams. The mythographer, Joseph Campbell said, 'the myth is to the collective as the dream is to the individual'; in other words the myth is communicating similar kinds of information that the dreamer is picking up from their unconscious – what Jungians would call 'archetypal' information. These are universal patterns which come from the collective unconscious. Both communicate using symbolism and these symbols may mean different things to different people.

There is a Maori myth of a chief called Kahukura whose tribe struggle to fish using lines, but are continually starving although the fish are plentiful.

Kahukura spends hours sitting by the shore thinking, and often others are resentful as they think he should be working alongside them. They think he is just sitting around. What they don't see is that he is engaged in a very creative process that requires time and space and if all his energy were devoted to fishing with the others this process could not take place.

Anyway, one night as he is sleeping, Kahukura has a dream of a long, white sandy beach on the other side of the island. In his dream he feels an urge to go and find this beach.

When he awakes he is determined to find the beach, although he doesn't know why.

Others are sceptical and see it as a wild goose chase, but off he goes. He travels all day until just as the sun is setting he pushes through some undergrowth and comes upon the beach of his dreams. He is filled with excitement and anticipation.

He waits as it begins to get dark and then he sees boats pull up on the shore and out come fairy people who are silvery and bright beings. They proceed to use a shimmering bag full of holes which they cast out into the sea and pull back laden with fish. The chief cannot believe what he is seeing and he knows that the thing will change the lives of his people for the better. He knows he must get one or find out how it is made.

So after some time Kahukura makes his way down on to the beach and mingles among the fairy people. He joins a group who are threading fish on a line by the gills so they can take them away in their boats. They are hurrying as someone has seen that the moon has gone down and the first streaks of light are appearing on the horizon. The chief knows he hasn't much time so what he does is very crafty. He undoes the knot at the end of the string so that as quickly as fish are threaded on, they come off at the end. This puts the people in disarray so that the sun has come up before they know it and they flee, leaving the fairy net on the sand.

The chief picks it up and takes it back to his people, who quickly work out how it is made and how to use it. They are able to catch large amounts of fish and the people of the village never go hungry again.

The feeling of anticipation and excitement when we get information from deep within is very satisfying. It is a feeling of connectedness, parts of ourselves just join together and we can operate from a much broader base than previously.

I have had experience of this several times and each time it was very thrilling.

I once had a request from a women's group to design a workshop that they could run for children who had witnessed violence in the home. When the request was made I had no ideas but I said I would think about it and get back to them.

The next day I was looking for a story for an elderly group so I took a copy of Grimm's fairy tales to read on the train. This was unusual in itself as it was rare that I used fairy stories with elderly groups.

I flicked through the book and began to read the story of 'Jack and the beanstalk' which I hadn't read for a very long time, and I was appalled at how violent it was. Jack makes three visits to the house of the giant and each time the giant returns the giant's wife hides him somewhere in the kitchen. From his secret vantage point Jack witnesses the giant returning and verbally and physically abusing his wife, eating and drinking and then falling fast asleep. On the third occasion, the giant awakes as Jack is making his escape and pursues Jack but cannot catch him because, 'he had drunk so much that he could not stand'.

It was at this point that the penny dropped for me and I sat in the train and felt the hairs go up on the back of my neck as I realised that on so many levels this story was a description of life as a child in the house of a violent and abusive father.

I designed a workshop for the group based around the story of Jack and the beanstalk and it went very well.

The other thing that is clear from both stories is that when someone makes such a journey it benefits us all. The chief's tribe and John's immediate family and community enjoy the results of their journey.

Using the story in a session

One of my co-therapists had inherited some wonderful things from a great aunt that we wanted to use in a session. These included some whalebone stays, packets of needles, very old and very immaculate, and a tortoiseshell comb. We thought these were perfect items for the pedlar's tray.

A lot of people could remember pedlars and people selling on the streets. Some people remembered Romanyies selling pegs and lucky charms and stories they were told of gypsy people stealing children! The stays caused much amusement and we had great fun trying them on. Most of the women remembered wearing them, with relief that they no longer had to.

The Three Dancing Princesses

Once there was a king who had three lovely daughters. They slept every night in one room with the door locked but every morning their shoes were discovered completely worn through and the girls would not say where they had been.

The king was desperate to get to the bottom of the mystery so he sent a proclamation throughout the kingdom that whoever could discover where the princesses went at night could have one for his wife. If the man failed he would forfeit his head and he had three nights to try.

Many men tried and many men failed and each lost his head as a result. Every morning there were the three pairs of shoes of the princesses with the leather completely worn through.

Now it so happened that an old soldier who had been wounded in battle was returning to his own land passed and through the kingdom and heard of the proclamation. He was on his way to the palace to try his luck when he came upon an old woman in a wood. She asked him where he was bound and he told her.

'Well,' she said, 'just take care not to drink any wine before you retire and here is a cloak which lends invisibility to whoever wears it.'

The old soldier thanked the old woman and made his way to the palace.

When he presented himself to the king there was much scepticism throughout the court at the prospect of an old man succeeding where younger men had failed. But that evening he was taken to the outer chamber of the room where the princesses slept and made himself ready to watch for the night.

Very soon, the eldest princess appeared with a goblet of wine which the old soldier took and pretended to drink.

A few moments later he made a great display of yawning and stretching and then began to feign sleep with loud snores.

When the princesses saw this they began to laugh and the eldest said, 'come, we must hurry'.

Then they dressed in their finest clothes and the eldest stood in front of her bed and clapped her hands. Her bed flew up to reveal a secret trapdoor into which the three disappeared.

Quick as a flash, the old soldier donned his magic cloak and crept after the girls. The trapdoor led to a flight of stairs and at the bottom there was a beautiful grove of trees with leaves of silver that glittered in the moonlight. As they were going through, the soldier snapped off a branch and hid it beneath his cloak.

Then they came to a grove of trees covered in leaves of gold and afterwards trees with leaves of diamonds, and each time the soldier snapped off a branch and hid it under his cloak.

Soon they came to a great lake and at the shore waited three little boats in which waited three princes. The princesses danced down to the shore and greeted the princes and got into the boats and they rowed off. The soldier got into one of the boats and was taken over to the other side where there were the bright lights of a castle and the sound of music and laughter.

There the three princesses and their princes danced until dawn, when the soles of their shoes were worn through and they had to leave.

The princes rowed them back across the lake and when they reached the other side the soldier ran ahead of them through the groves and up the stairs to the trapdoor so he could arrange himself in bed as if he had never moved.

When the princesses came in, the eldest came over to look at the soldier who was snoring loudly and said to the others: 'I don't think we are going to have to worry about this one'.

Then they pulled off their fine dresses and worn-out dancing slippers and fell into bed.

The next two nights the soldier went with them again, always undetected in the old woman's invisible cloak. On the third occasion he took a goblet from the banqueting hall as further proof of where he had been.

On the morning of the third day the old soldier was summoned to the court and asked by the king, 'do you know where my daughters go at night?'.

To everyone's astonishment the soldier replied, 'yes, my liege. Your daughters go with three princes to a castle under the ground'.

With that the old soldier produced the branch of silver and one of gold and one of diamonds and the goblet he had taken from the banqueting hall.

The king called for his daughters and when they heard the old soldier's story they knew they were discovered and so confessed everything.

The king asked the soldier which daughter he would like to marry and he said, 'I am not young so I will have the eldest'.

And so they were married and the soldier ruled the kingdom after the king's death.

Themes in the story

This story is often known as 'The twelve dancing princesses' but I thought I would probably have a problem casting twelve so I decreased it to three. (There is a version from Paderborn, Westphalia, which has three princesses.)

The old soldier is an unlikely hero and I tend to emphasise that in the story to make his subsequent success even more satisfying. He is also returning from war, wounded. The story is presenting someone who really doesn't have a lot going for him. It is unlikely he will be going to war again. Yet by the end of the story he is married to a princess and about to inherit a kingdom!

There is also an old woman in the story in a now familiar role of mysterious helpmeet. Without her help it is unlikely that the old soldier would have fared any better than his predecessors. She tells him not to drink the drugged wine which the princesses will offer him. The motif of a drugged drink is very common in stories and often cautions the hero against a loss of consciousness or awareness (see 'The black bull of Norway' Chapter 6). It is significant that the drink is offered by the princesses – the hero must not let himself get distracted by the youth and beauty of the people he has come to watch. The cloak of invisibility is interesting in the light of what I have said about the 'invisibility' of elderly people within our communities.

Using the story in a session

I once used this story with a group which included people with a real range of abilities. One woman was particularly fond of dancing and quite often at the end of a session a couple of the women would get up and dance with each other and the care assistants. This is one reason I particularly wanted to find a story that contained dancing. Others in the group were quite disabled, with one man in a wheelchair and one woman very confused.

I had just returned from holiday in Turkey, where I had bought a pair of brocade slippers with pointed toes which I wanted to show people. I had a pair of Japanese wooden shoes that I had picked up from a jumble sale, so I used these as objects in the story which emphasises the worn-out dancing shoes. I had also brought back some Turkish Delight which I wanted to share with people, so I included it in the story by saying that the princesses brought the old soldier some wine and a few pieces of a delicious sweetmeat!

The shoes stimulated a great deal of discussion and one of the care assistants put the Japanese shoes on and hobbled around.

I asked people what different kinds of dances they danced. They mentioned the fox-trot, jitterbug, jive, waltz and tango. Elsie, who loved dancing, even demonstrated some of the steps. Encouraged by the residents, Grace, one of the care assistants, showed us an African dance that was very graceful and involved much gyrating from the hips. Some of the residents got up to try, even Nancy who held on to her zimmer frame as she did it.

George wanted to play the old soldier because, he said, 'I am an old soldier'.

Elsie was the eldest princess, with Nancy and Grace as her sisters. Margaret, who was often in very low spirits, played the old woman in the forest. I was really pleased, as she often declined to play a part as she didn't feel up to it. I asked the other care assistant to play all three princes and George laughed and said, 'she'll have to work really hard to row that lot across!'.

During the enactment, one woman who was watching leaned across to me and said, 'you know, my father would never let us go to dances either. We used to have to sneak out and say we were going somewhere else'.

In this way she was identifying with the princesses and making personal connections with an element in the story that was about maintaining a life separate and secret from the authoritative parent.

At the end of the session as the stabiliser we 'danced' at the wedding of the old soldier and the eldest princess and then role played slipping off our dancing shoes and fine clothes.

4

The Theme of Loss in the Lives of Elderly People

According to Jung, the task of the first forty years of life was to establish oneself in the world, to work, raise a family and take our place in society. The task of the second half of life was much more introspective. It involved looking inward and integrating life experiences, including our relationship with ourselves and others. His view of old age was one of contemplation and spirituality and the possibility of a resolution of the issues we grapple with throughout our lives.

Not everyone has such a positive view of old age, in fact, as I have said, it is commonly the contrary. When I was training as a drama therapist we had to choose placements where, accompanied by a tutor and in small groups, we practised our new skills and shared our experiences with the whole group afterwards. The choice of placement included working with adults with autism, physically disabled children, with a group in a psychiatric day centre and with behaviourally disturbed adolescents. It also included working with an elderly group of people who had had strokes and were physically very frail, but there was very little enthusiasm for this placement. Each week the students who had this placement reported back despondently about their sessions. They spoke of how much the experience stimulated their own feelings and fears about growing old. They realised they lacked an understanding of the process of ageing and that a lot of their fears stemmed from ignorance. They had to work really hard to stimulate interest and energy.

This group was in the final stages of life. According to Erickson[1], who devised a model of personality development based on eight stages, old age is characterised by the polarities of ego integrity versus despair. By this he meant that a person had to come to terms with the choices they had made in their life and the consequences of those choices and accept the reality of having only one life. This he called 'ego integrity'. If the person wasn't able to do this they faced despair. The issues were around completion and resolution – but how to work with these when people regularly fell asleep or were paralysed down one side or couldn't speak? Gradually the placement students began to adapt their methods to suit the client group. They began to form relationships with members of the group. They experimented and observed, and developed any little initiative that came from the individuals in the group. They began to find the work rewarding.

The theme of loss is one of the central issues when working with elderly people and yet some people who work in this field seek to avoid it altogether. There are many reasons for this. It could have to do with the individual's own feelings towards this issue, the atmosphere prevailing in the place in which they work and wider society's attitude towards death.

We live in a culture that is death denying and yet I have never met an elderly person who was in the slightest bit self-conscious about death. In some residential homes death is talked about freely with residents and people are encouraged to speak of what they would like for their funeral or any bequests they have to make. This is a very healthy state of affairs and I have known residents who loved to be able to talk and to make plans with a trusted person of what they wanted to happen after their death.

Many cultures look with horror on the prospect of a death going unremarked and unremembered, yet that is often what happens in hospitals and nursing homes up and down the country. I have trained staff for whom this was a distressing state of affairs. They have wanted to honour particular residents and pay their respects but the policy of the place in which they work forbids it. Sometimes there was a real lack of sensitivity informing staff about a resident's death, often ignoring the depth of the bond between them. I have heard stories of the death of a resident being kept from other residents as if it were something shameful to be kept secret.

To refuse to acknowledge death is to ignore life. Not to acknowledge a person's passing is not to acknowledge their life, and death gives a wonderful opportunity to remember and salute a person.

1   Erik Erickson (1963) *Childhood and Society*. New York: W.W. Naughton.

We all want to be remembered. I always made a point of mentioning someone's death if they had been a member of a group. I would say how much I would miss them and dedicate the session to them.

An old lady we were very fond of died and we attended her funeral. She had been a very enthusiastic member of the story group and would often remember stories from one week to the next. She had no friends or family at the funeral, only staff from the hospital where she had lived for the last five years of her life. She had not been a regular church goer so was not familiar to the priest who conducted the service. I really wanted an opportunity to say how special she had been to us. We told the story of Eagle and Coyote at the service (see below). The next week we used the story in the group of which she had been a member and told people about her funeral. This lady had shared a room with three other ladies, none of whom she was very close to but who knew she had died. The people she was closest to were friends in other parts of the hospital who she met up with at various activities and they had not been informed of her death. It was really good to give people an opportunity to say how sorry they were that she'd died. We were also communicating to the group that every member was special and that we would notice their absence and miss their presence.

I once turned up for a session to be told that Lily, a regular member of the group, was in a coma and not expected to live long. Lily came to the sessions every single week with her daughter, Violet, who organised her visiting times to coincide with the sessions as she loved stories too. I went up to see Lily in her room after the session and Violet was there. She told me that her mum was very poorly 'but was hanging on'. Together we sat beside the bed as Lily lay in a very deep coma. I asked Violet if Lily could hear anything and she said she had been told not but she thought she could. I asked Violet what she thought about me telling Lily the story we had used in the session and her face lit up. She said, 'I think mum would love that'. I began by telling Lily she had been sorely missed in the session and that I had a story I thought she might like. I then told her the story I had used earlier with the group, which was the story of Gilgamesh. It is a very moving story of striving and struggling and eventually letting go of the quest for immortality. The lady in the next bed told me, 'she can't hear you, dear', but we carried on, Violet holding and stroking her mum's hand while I leaned close and told the story. Lily died the following day and I was really glad I had had the opportunity to say goodbye to her in this way.

So let's have a look at this issue in more detail and examine its significance both for our clients and ourselves.

In training sessions I begin to approach the subject of loss by suggesting a 'brainstorm'. This is a way of accessing the broadest amount of information on any given subject and utilising the resources of the team by asking everybody to contribute. It involves writing on a flip chart all the examples of loss the people in the group can think of.

Usually the first thing people mention is death but the brainstorm encourages us to explore how far-reaching and much more personal our experience of loss can be.

Many people, including myself, can reach quite a mature age without experiencing a major bereavement, in other words the loss of a significant person in their lives. I know in my own case that this was the result of living in a family that did not have much, if any, contact with members of the extended family. So both sets of grandparents died when I was quite small, but I hadn't had sufficient contact with them for it to register as a loss. I experienced this much more as an absence which resurfaced as an adult when I began to work with elderly people and developed very loving relationships with certain individuals which I found very satisfying. I felt that one of the reasons for this was that they were in some way substituting for the grandparents I never had.

Loss can take the form of a bereavement, including miscarriage and abortion, a divorce or a separation.

It can also be the loss of possessions, either accidentally losing something or through the actions of another, for example a burglary or a mugging. We may then experience feelings of loss of personal safety or security.

A disappointment is a loss, what you've lost is the possibility of something. Sometimes people say, 'I don't want to get excited about it because if it doesn't happen I'll be disappointed'. That's how much people want to avoid disappointment and it's because of its link with loss.

Moving to another country, even if it's to avoid intolerable living conditions in your own country, involves loss of a homeland.

Potentially positive events involve loss at some level. Most major life changes involve loss – moving house, changing jobs, getting married, having a baby. Researchers at the university of the West of England believe that post-natal depression could be a form of grieving for a lost lifestyle. Doctors have failed to discover a link between post-natal depression and hormone levels or other physical factors, implying the condition is psychological in origin.[2] It is no coincidence that the above events figure largely in the stress tables researchers devised to assess the levels of stress involved in specific life events.

When we are younger there may be more of a balance between the amount of loss we experience and other new things that are flowing in to replace or camouflage the loss. At any age, people can experience a huge imbalance, say, for example, when they have a string of bereavements of significant people, they lose their job or their marriage begins to founder. This can place an intolerable strain on people which they may need support to get through.

I then ask people to think for a moment and write down a list of all the losses they can think of in their own life. These are not necessarily the most recent. Events that happened years ago may still be having a huge impact.

People then have a chance to talk about their list with a partner, and I ask people to notice what that feels like. Some people find it a relief to talk, others find it very difficult. I have had people begin a course saying they are really eager to talk about and explore loss, yet when we begin to do so they encounter huge resistance. In this way, we begin to learn about our own responses to grief and loss.

I ask people to explore this further by thinking about how they like to be treated when they are grieving. Some people like to be left alone, some people like to talk and cry and be held, some people like to be alone but know that others are around. We discover that there are a number of different responses to grief and that there is no right or wrong way.

I then ask people to think about how they respond to others who are grieving. Very often, people's response to others reflects the way they respond to themselves and how they like to be treated when they are grieving – we do unto others what we would like to have done to ourselves. Although it's understandable this is not always appropriate – I may not want to talk about grief when I have suffered a loss but I may have a resident who is desperate to talk or express their grief in some way.

What happens if we don't talk about or express feelings in some way is that they start to accumulate charge around them which as it is not being discharged starts to feel enormous or overwhelming. This can result in a vicious circle because the person who is frightened of expressing feelings stores them up, they then start to feel overwhelmed and then become even more frightened so hang on to them even more. They can develop catastrophic fantasies about what would happen if they expressed their feelings. People tell me, 'I don't let myself cry because if I did I would never stop'. And because they never let themselves, they don't have the chance to test out this hypothesis in reality.

When we allow much more of a flow between feeling and expression we experience less anxiety and we observe our feelings change and flow and move on. We also become more comfortable around the feelings of others. One of the fears that people have about exploring issues of loss with their residents is that the residents will get upset. Underlying this is often a fear that they will get upset. The other fear around residents getting upset is that as the worker it is their job to somehow fix it. Clearly this is not possible and the following stories offer ideas for alternative approaches.

I then ask people to brainstorm with me all the possible losses experienced by elderly people.

When we begin to speculate on the losses experienced by our elderly clients, we soon discover that they are in the position of experiencing loss on a massive scale without the solace or excitement of new things coming in to replace the things lost.

These are some of the possible losses and you may think of more.

1. *Physical or health losses.* A natural consequence of ageing is some level of sensory loss. Not all of the senses are affected to the same extent, so my hearing may be poor but my sight remains acute. Moreover, the speed that a sense deteriorates may vary. The repercussions of sensory loss are enormous. If my hearing is poor I will find it much more difficult to hold a conversation or take part in a discussion. I will be easily startled because I won't hear people coming up behind me. I may have loved music and that is now ruined for me. If my sight is poor I may not recognise people. I may be very unsteady on my feet because the room is a blur. Reading or watching television becomes impossible. I will lose confidence in my ability to move around unassisted because of a fear of falling.

   One of the ways I explore this in training is through a series of simple exercises that are designed to impair a person's functions in some way for a very brief period of time to allow them to experience the consequences of sensory loss for themselves. People are given industrial goggles smeared with Vaseline to imitate visual loss and ear plugs to dull their hearing. They are escorted around the room by two others who are instructed to interact with each other rather than the 'disabled' person in their care. Within minutes, people experience a range of very powerful emotions such as anger and despair. They adapt themselves accordingly, perhaps by collapsing and 'giving up', which is reflected in their body language and demeanour. Their shoulders slump, they drag their feet, they are unsteady and easily unbalanced or they become rigid and stiff, often pulling backwards with their head up. People are given rubber gloves which they wear while trying to feel the skin on another's hand and to perform a simple task which the presence of the gloves makes frustratingly difficult. In this way, our understanding becomes felt as well as theoretical, and hopefully increases the amount of sensitivity we have when we interact with that person.

A stroke may result in paralysis down one or both sides which may or may not be permanent. It may affect the person's sight, speech and mobility. Depending on its severity, it will influence every aspect of the person's life, from their ability to feed themselves to whether they still have control over their bladder and bowels. The person's mental faculties may be just as acute as they always were. They may have to cope with feelings of shame and frustration and a loss of dignity, independence and autonomy. Depression is very common, particularly directly after the stroke as the person works to adjust to their change in circumstances. There is also extreme anxiety as the person fears further strokes. I have seen people struggle to come to terms with the effects of a stroke, sometimes working hard to regain some of what's been lost only to suffer another stroke.

2. *Financial and material losses.* Elderly people often suffer loss of income when they retire and have to survive on a pension. The person may lose their own home and a great deal of furniture and other precious belongings when they move into residential care. They may experience a loss of their own space, sometimes sharing a room with other people. Disability may bring an extreme loss of

personal space and dignity, for example the person may need assistance to wash and go to the loo.

An elderly person may also experience the loss of being in charge of their own money. Money is power and a lot of people would associate having control over their own finances as a major part of being an adult. With the move into residential care, the person has to develop a different relationship with money. The day-to-day handling of their finances is often done by a member of staff within the organisation. It also means that opportunities to spend money are few. It is unlikely that the elderly person will be able to pop out to the shops when they feel like it, and in fact shopping becomes a major activity and expedition in itself.

3. *Loss of social standing and status that goes with having a trade or a valued role such as mother.* This is a major loss that is often underestimated. We know of the high incidence of men dying soon after retirement and yet we continue to fantasise about how great it would be to win the lottery and never have to work again. A large part of our self-esteem comes from the work we do, as well as it creating structure in our lives and providing varied relationships. Most people grew up with the work ethic which said 'you are what you can do' – how often have we heard men who have been laid off refer to themselves as 'on the scrapheap'? Raising a family and being the homemaker was previously one of the few ways a woman had of acquiring status, and in some cultures this is still the case. There is more recognition of what a loss this can be for a woman with the creation of the term 'empty nest syndrome'.

In one residential home I visited, the kitchen was out of bounds for all of the residents except for one woman who used to help with the washing up and do minor chores. The staff had discovered that without this outlet the level of the woman's anxiety was intolerably high. In this way they recognised the importance of the mothering role to her and created opportunities for her to enact it.

4. *Loss of cognitive abilities and the ability to think.* This can mean that previously simple tasks are beyond our capabilities. Our use of language may be impaired. We may be unable to construct or understand simple sentences. We may lose short- and medium-term memory which will have a huge effect on our feelings of

familiarity and security. Can you imagine looking around you and not knowing where you are? Being surrounded by strangers and people who have very odd behaviour? I'm talking about the elderly person in a special unit for people with dementia. That person doesn't think to themselves, 'I have dementia, that is why I'm in this place surrounded by other people with dementia'. Inside they feel the way they've always felt and can often be alarmed at people talking to themselves or acting in a bizarre way.

Memory loss means a person might not remember a surviving spouse, or recognise them in the case of visual agnosia. Sometimes, although the person has very little short-term memory their long-term memory is good. What this can mean is that they grieve again for people lost years before because the memories are so vivid compared with more recent memories. So much of memory informs identity – our memories of who we were in the past give a substance and a context to who we are now.

5.   *Loss of spouse and life-long partner.* When a person goes into residential care they may have slept beside the same person every night for forty or fifty years. Occasionally couples go into residential care together and sometimes homes make provision for them by providing them with a room together. However, this is not always the case.

6.   *Loss of family and friends.* I was often astounded by how few of the people I worked with had visitors.

7.   *Loss of freedom and independence and autonomy.* The person may have lost mobility or be living in residential care, or both. In training I ask people to write down all the choices they have made from the moment they woke up until now. People who think of themselves as not having many choices are surprised at how many they have. Choices over what to wear, what to have for breakfast, which route to take, who to sit beside. I then ask them to consider the choices of their clients and residents, and they are often struck by how limited those choices are.

I ask people what they feel when they look at the picture of loss that emerges. Often people feel sad or depressed. Some people say they feel afraid. In some ways we are looking at a possible future for ourselves and that is important to recognise. The purpose of the exercise is awareness – not just of the elderly person's position but of our own feelings towards them. For me it is really important that we are aware of these feelings because they will influence the way we work with people in this stage of life.

In his introduction to *On Death and Dying*, C. Murray Parkes says:

> A well rounded life should have a beginning, a middle and an end. Not just for reasons of symmetry but because, though I may be mortal, the social system of which I am part is immortal and my arrival into and departure from that social system are important events which need to be prepared for.[3]

Stories are a really good model for this because every story has a beginning, a middle and an end, and the format of the sessions also reflects this.

Even the simplest story structures rely on an ending. A joke is a story that doesn't work without a punchline. A soap opera manages by the existence of interweaving story lines to sustain interest while acknowledging the need for endings. So one story line may wind itself up (and depending on the character and style of ending provide a huge amount of interest) while another carries on.

Myths in particular concern themselves with existential questions of the nature of life and death (unlike some folk and fairy tales which are much more concerned with how to find a partner and have a comfortable life). They explore these questions in a way that is very intriguing and emotionally engaging. So instead of saying 'death is very final and very mysterious', the story says, 'the land of the living is on one side and the land of the dead on the other. They are separated by a river and the land of the dead is covered in swirling mists'.

The wonderful thing about story is that you can work with issues such as death in a very oblique and sensitive way. Because it is clearly a story, set in a landscape that is far away and long ago, a person can choose whether to identify with the characters or issues or not. In this way it is a very non-confrontational way of working. You do not have to use stories that involve actual deaths, and indeed of the stories I have included here only one deals with death in an overt way ('Coyote and Eagle') and this focuses on people's responses to death rather than the death itself.

3   Elisabeth Kubler-Ross (1970) *On Death and Dying.* London: Tavistock.

I refer to the themes in a story to alert you to the possibilities of your clients resonating with different aspects of a story. It is important not to assume that because clients are elderly they will identify with an elderly position. It is possible they will identify with anyone in the story (another good reason not to hoist roles on to people but to offer them a choice). Because our experience of loss is not chronological, a client may be taken back to unresolved loss from childhood. When working with the story of Demeter and Persephone I often ask groups, 'if you had to choose between your husband and your mother, whom would you choose?'. I have always been shocked at how many people unequivocally choose their mother. One woman told me, 'you can have another husband but you only have one mother'. Stories offer the possibility of resolving issues from a much earlier period in the person's life.

A story can raise an issue imaginatively which is described in terms of symbol. Symbol is the language of the unconscious so a story can then be taken in on an unconscious level.

Story sessions provide opportunities to explore issues of loss and resolution with people who are unable or do not wish to process the experience verbally. For those who have lost verbal comprehension through a dementing illness or a stroke, the story session can offer a way of addressing this issue in a way that can be understood on an emotional and experiential level. So for example, in the limber we may explore this somatically in a form of exercise that involves holding on and letting go. An enactment of a story such as Demeter and Persephone gives the opportunity to watch or enact the character of Demeter as she searches for, and eventually is reunited with, her lost child.

Demeter and Persephone

There was a time when it was eternally summer. The earth was looked after by an earth goddess called Demeter. Under her protection and guidance the crops grew, the rivers flowed and babies were born. All good things came from her bounty.

Demeter had a daughter who she dearly loved. She was called Persephone and was twelve or thirteen years old, a little thing just on the brink of womanhood.

One day Persephone was playing by herself picking flowers on the Vale of Enna when there was a rumble from below the earth. Suddenly the ground split open and out came Hades, the king of the underworld, on his huge black horse. Seeing the girl, he galloped over, threw her over the pommel of his horse, reared about and disappeared into the underworld. The ground closed behind him, leaving no trace of the girl.

That evening Demeter came calling for her daughter. She searched high and low but there was no sign of the girl. Everywhere she went she asked frantically if anyone had seen her daughter. She called for her until her throat was hoarse. Finally, after much searching, she came back to the spot where her daughter had disappeared. There she learnt from the stream nymph who inhabited a stream that flows into the underworld that her daughter was with Hades, god of the underworld. 'She sits on a throne and looks very sad but very regal,' said the nymph.

Demeter was furious that Hades had abducted her daughter and made her his bride. She sat down on the ground and refused to work until her daughter was returned to her.

Very soon the people began to experience great hardship. The rivers stopped flowing, the crops were stunted in the fields and the grape withered on the vine. For the first time famine came to the land.

Starving, the people chose representatives to go and beg Zeus, the chief and most powerful god, to intervene. Zeus was in a delicate position as Hades was his brother and he did not wish to alienate him. So he instructed the god Hermes to intercede on his behalf.

Hermes was the winged messenger god, fleet of foot and quick of tongue. He flew down into the underworld to speak to Hades and try to get him to release Persephone. Hades, however, had grown very fond of her and she was now his wife. It took a lot to get him to give her up but eventually he reluctantly agreed.

Hermes prepared to take Persephone back to the upper air to be reunited with her mother. However, he remembered an ancient rule of the underworld. He asked her, 'Have you eaten anything while you have been here?'. Persephone shook her head then suddenly remembered. 'Oh yes, but only six pomegranate seeds'. Hermes thought deeply for a moment. He knew that it was unlawful to eat of the food of the underworld and leave. His quick mind created a compromise and he announced it to all assembled: 'For every pomegranate seed you will spend one month here with your husband. The remaining six months you will spend with your mother above ground. Where do you wish to go first?'. Persephone replied, 'I have missed my mother and wish to see her'. 'So be it,' said Hermes, who whisked her out of the underworld to a joyful reunion with her mother.

In her happiness Demeter once again released her bounty on the world. The crops grew, the rivers flowed and summer returned. When the time came for Persephone to return to her husband, Demeter mourned once more and winter arrived in the land. But from then on the people knew that although the winter might be long and arduous, after six months Persephone would return to her mother and spring would come again to the world in all its glory.

Themes in the story

This is a story I have used with a variety of different elderly groups, including people with a dementia. It has very easily identifiable characters and many concrete images. The actions are striking and sometimes shocking, the abduction, the searching, the journeying back and forth from upper air to underworld. The narrative structure is simple.

This story works on so many levels it is worth coming back to again and again. On one level it is a very early explanation of the seasons and a reassurance in the dead of winter that spring will come again. It is one reason why I often use the story in the autumn or early winter.

On another level it describes a mother's struggle to let go of her daughter so that she can have a husband and a life of her own. The mother/daughter relationship is described as very close and idyllic. It will take an outside intervention of some force to separate them. The story portrays this in the violent abduction by Hades (in many versions of the story the abduction is accompanied by Hades' rape of Persephone but this is a feature I deliberately remove when I use this story with elderly groups).

The story emphasises the struggle of an individual to separate from 'mother' and make their own way in the world, referring to Persephone prior to her abduction as the 'kore', which is a generic term meaning maiden. Thus she clearly does not have an identity of her own other than a very general one. She only becomes known as Persephone when she is queen of the underworld and the story is careful to point out that this is a role that she has assumed and is convincing in (the nymph tells Demeter that she has seen her daughter sitting on the throne looking sad 'but very regal'). She then appears in other myths as a goddess in her own right.

On another level the story could be said to describe the loss of childhood and all that this signifies in terms of innocence, playfulness and a merging with mother. This can be seen in the character of Persephone and it is also reiterated in the effect of Demeter's loss on the people of the earth. The story begins with a description of the world as a place that is forever summer, where bounty flows, seemingly without anyone having to make any effort. This is a very childlike state. The famine that ensues from Demeter's grief is a rude awakening for people and they need help in order to survive. They ask Zeus, who is the 'father' god, for help. In this way they begin to move from the domain of the mother (which is being nurtured and looked after) to that of the father, which is about taking one's place in the world. The people in the story have to grow up.

Even when some semblance of order is returned with the institution of the seasons, reassurance is needed that summer and abundance will return.

I can't think of any story that does not present the idea of the underworld as a potentially hazardous place to be feared and exceptionally vigilant in. Inanna in the Babylonian myth gives instructions to her handmaiden that if she is not back in three days to raise a hue and cry in the hall of the gods and come and rescue her. Orpheus is given very precise information on what to do in the underworld in order to reclaim Eurydice. He falters and loses her forever. Psyche's last task is a visit to the underworld (coincidentally to get some ointment from Persephone). She has to take cakes to distract Cerberus, the three-headed dog, and coins to pay the ferryman over the River Styx. Persephone disappears into the underworld a girl and in the course of the story she matures into a woman with great power. (Persephone as a goddess was associated with supernatural powers and psychic ability.) The story makes psychological sense – we know we don't attain maturity without a struggle.

The struggle is also one of the things that makes the resolution so satisfying. All stories have some kind of resolution which we may not like but we can recognise their wisdom. The idyllic image at the beginning of the story can never be returned to, but the story creates a compromise which acknowledges the change that has occurred and which all the major players can live with.

On another level the story gives a very accurate portrayal of the different stages of loss. (Elizabeth Kubler-Ross identified these stages as denial, anger, bargaining, depression and acceptance. She was talking specifically about the stages that people who know they are dying go through and she recognised that there was a great deal of individual variation.)[4]

Demeter begins by searching for what she has lost, and when she has exhausted all her attempts she becomes very depressed and very angry. She is also impervious to other people's loss, that is, the effect of the famine on the people of the earth. She sits down and refuses to budge and after a while she is unable to move.

On one level the story is describing the progress of a depression, with the image of the person stuck in the underworld a very concrete symbol. In the Babylonian myth, when Inanna gets stuck in the underworld (she is killed by Erishkigal), a state of stasis ensues similar to this story when Persephone gets stuck in the underworld because Hades will not let her go. All growth in the upper world is stopped.

There is deadlock at this point. What breaks the deadlock is someone who comes from outside the immediate situation. In this the story conveys an important psychological truth and one that gives information on how to respond to a depression, our own or other people's.

If we see the person stuck in the underworld as a symbol of a depressed person, then how the story orchestrates their release is of vital importance. When the people ask Zeus for help what he does not do is send an army down to the underworld to rescue Persephone or order Hades to give her up. Both of these strategies would only have served to intensify Hades' resistance and he would probably have held on even more strongly. No, what Zeus did was to send someone subtle and persuasive, someone fleet of foot and mind

---

4   *On Death and Dying*; see note 3.

(to the Romans, Hermes was known as Mercury which is where the word 'mercurial' comes from). We don't know exactly what Hermes said to Hades but it worked.

In the story of Inanna, her lifeless body is rescued from the bowels of the underworld by two little sprites who are small and inconspicuous enough to slip down into the underworld unseen. There they spend much time with the goddess of the underworld, Erishkigal, who has killed Inanna and has possession of her body. Erishkigal is in great travail. The story is unclear whether this is grief or childbirth, but it is the sprites' approach to her suffering that is important. They spend days simply mirroring her distress. When she groans, 'oh, my outside is hurting' they groan, 'oh, my outside is hurting'. When she cries, 'oh, my inside is hurting' they cry, 'oh, my inside is hurting'. In this way the grief of Erishkigal is assuaged and she is so grateful that she agrees to release Inanna.

So often people think they have to do something special with someone when they are distressed or depressed rather than just be with them, listen to their distress, give good attention and be available for contact with them.

Using the story in a session

I used this story with quite a new group who were mostly in wheelchairs although there was one man who was mobile and blind. We usually sat in a semi-circle, although the limber in this session required us to sit in a circle. I had one regular assistant and one who came periodically but was very good.

If you're in a wheelchair all the time apart from when you're in bed your spatial awareness is impaired because you are always on mid level, never down on the ground or up in the air. This story contains a symbolic journey from the upper air to underground, so I used the limber to explore that idea somatically.

I did this by bringing in a piece of bright blue lycra which we stretched between us in the circle. Most clients only have the use of one hand but often that hand is very strong and has a good grip. I had two assistants and they positioned themselves beside the people who might have more trouble hanging on to the lycra. We were able to stretch the material very tight. I then threw a couple of bean bags on to the surface of the lycra and we practised bouncing them as high as we could, which was really good fun and stimulated lots of ooohs and aaahs and squealing. I then removed the bean bags and we tried to raise the lycra as high as we could, which gave people a really good stretch. We then tried to hold the lycra as close to the ground as we could, which was more difficult but possible. Finally, we stretched it out as much as we could at waist level and on the count of three let it go. In this way the limber also addressed issues of loss around holding on and letting go.

The objects I brought in were two pomegranates and a handful of fallen leaves (I did the session in October). Very often in old people's homes they have a board in the foyer which says what day it is and the date and what the weather is like outside. With the combined difficulties of moving people in a wheelchair and a lack of staff, it becomes very rare that a person goes outside the building. Their world becomes narrower and narrower and more and more artificial. People may know it is autumn but what can convey the season better than the sight, smell, sound and feel of a fallen leaf?

I cut up one of the pomegranates so that people could see what it looked like inside and took the other one round whole. I also gave people the opportunity to try the gem-like seeds.

I told the story and then asked if anyone wanted to play Demeter, the nature goddess, who produces the crops and all manner of good things. Lily said straight away, 'go on then, I'll do it'. As the group was quite new I asked my assistant, Adie, to play Persephone. She was an African nurse who was a great favourite with the residents. She immediately went and sat beside Lily and the two held hands. Barry, my regular assistant, played Hades and Michael immediately put his hand up when I asked for someone to play the chief god, Zeus. Rose offered to play Hermes. Everyone else was happy to play people and I thought I would wait until the enactment to see if anyone offered to be the spokesperson to ask Zeus for help.

The story began with a very loving portrayal of a mother and her daughter by Lily and Adie. Barry played Hades almost as a music hall villain, carrying off Adie squealing. I pushed Lily in her wheelchair as she went about asking if anyone had seen her daughter. It was a great moment when Doris as the river nymph said, 'yes, I have seen your daughter, love'. We got really excited and said 'where, where?'. Doris said, 'he got her, that chap, whatisname'. Lily, who has a brilliant memory, said 'do you mean Hades?' and Doris said, 'yes, that's him'.

When the people went to Zeus for help Emma spoke on their behalf and raised her hands out to the god in a gesture of pitiful supplication. 'We're so hungry,' she said. Michael played an unexpectedly compassionate Zeus, who initially wanted to go and get the girl himself but was persuaded to send Rose as Hermes. Rose often offered to play parts and when it was her cue would look at me and ask, 'what have I got to do?'. I would then explain the situation to her and let her take it from there. On this occasion she leaned forward to take Hades'/Barry's hand and said, 'let her go, her mum wants to see her'.

The reunion between Demeter and Persephone was clapped by the group. In the stabiliser I went round everyone using their real name and thanking them for the parts they played in the story. I played music and we had some hand dancing. Lily jokingly referred to Adie as her daughter for several weeks.

Coyote and Eagle

Coyote goes to see his friend Eagle, who is grieving for the loss of his wife who has just died. 'Why do these things happen?' asks Eagle. Coyote is sad to see his friend so unhappy so he suggests they go to the land of the dead to get Eagle's wife back. Eagle eagerly agrees.

A river divides the land of the living from the land of the dead. Eagle and Coyote stand on the banks and look across to the land of the dead wreathed in mist and shadows. They find a canoe in the reeds and paddle across.

On the other shore stands an old woman who beckons them to her. Without a word she takes them to a hut, feeds them rice and chicken and shuts them in. Resourceful as ever, Coyote takes a chicken bone and rips a hole in the hide. He makes a needle from the bone and with hair from the hide he sews a bag from the piece of hide.

Together Eagle and Coyote slip through the hole and out into the mists and swirling spirits. They run with the bag open and gather up spirits in the bags including the spirit of Eagle's wife and the old woman.

They paddle back to the land of the living and joyfully open the bag to celebrate the return of Eagle's wife. However, the old woman shakes her head. 'No,' she says, 'we cannot remain here'. Eagle's wife tells him, 'we do not belong here. All things must pass. But be assured, we will meet again'. With that the spirits depart and are lost in the swirling mists. Coyote takes his friend's arm and they make their way back to their village.

Themes in the story

There are many, many stories of characters unsuccessfully trying to cheat death. The hero Gilgamesh actually attains the holy watercress of immortality after arduous adventures, only to lose it to the skin-shedding snake (who ancient peoples believed was immortal). In the Irish tale, Oisin tries to stay forever young but fails. Both Demeter in Greek mythology and Isis in Egyptian mythology try to confer immortality on young children. On both occasions the sacred rites they use in order to do this are interrupted and so are unsuccessful. Achilles' mother, Thetis, made all but his heel invulnerable by dipping him in the River Styx but he was killed by an arrow in the heel. What these stories are doing is emphasising a basic fact of life – that everyone must die. It is very often human nature to know that but to deny it. The story of Coyote and Eagle looks at what happens when we deny the reality of death.

The character of Coyote in this North American Indian story is a trickster. His trickery on this occasion is a lot about not wanting to see his dear friend grieve. This is a very common reaction towards another person's loss and their subsequent distress. It may take the form of jollying someone out of their grief or trying to move them on before they're ready. It can often come from discomfort that we experience in relation to our own grief.

The story shows Coyote's efforts to be misguided. In some ways a person's grieving time may be prolonged by another's encouragement to deny the reality of the loss.

The story could mirror the experience of someone in your group in that Eagle's wife has died and you may have someone who has recently lost a spouse. The story has an other worldly quality that puts it clearly in a mythical space, but you may choose not to use it at this time. The emphasis is more on Eagle's response to his wife's death and those around him rather than the death itself. It is a very powerful story and it will probably evoke a lot of thoughts and feelings.

Using the story in a session

The group has a range of different abilities. A couple of the women are very able with a good level of fitness, one woman seems to be dementing, several women are very frail and have frames, and one man is in a wheelchair. The group has been running every week for eight weeks and I have at least two helpers from the staff who are always very enthusiastic and animated.

The group get a great deal of enjoyment out of interacting with their staff in this way and the staff have a tradition of singing and dancing for the residents and making them laugh.

Some members of the group had been doing keep fit classes up until very recently and they are very enthusiastic about the limber. Edith can do high kicks. I stress that we each do what is comfortable and I lead a physical limber sitting down. I go methodically through the body, starting by rubbing the hands together and then taking the warmth to the arms and the shoulders and then to the knees and the thighs and down the calves as far as is comfortable.

The objects I bring in are a couple of drums. One is an Irish buran, which is a wide flat drum with crossbars at the back with which you hold the drum while you play it with a stick. It looks a little like a Native American drum. The other is a pair of bongos which can sit very nicely on a person's lap. Some people really bang the drum, some people beat out a rhythm. One woman very gently traces her finger nails across the skin, making the most delicate of sounds. She seems really to like the buran and holds it on her lap throughout the story.

I tell the story first while Grace, the staff member, repeats some of it to Nellie, who is hard of hearing. At the end Edith sighs and says, 'what a lovely story'.

This is a group that are usually very proactive in choosing roles and when I ask 'who would like to do what?' George immediately says, 'I'll play the chap whose wife has died'. Grace offers to play Eagle, which is a good way to support George in his role, and Edith wants to play the mysterious wise woman in the land of the spirits. Belinda, the other staff member, offers to play Eagle's wife and everyone else in the group opts to be spirits. Mark, another staff member, turns up at this point and is very jokey and boisterous, which is initially quite jarring but as soon as we give him a role he settles down and gets really absorbed in the story. (Edith suggested he was the river that divided the land of the living from the land of the dead.)

George and Grace play their parts beautifully. When they come to cross the river Grace sits behind George's wheelchair and pushes gently while he 'paddles'. She pushes him around the room when they run with the bag gathering up spirits. Edith is stately and authoritative as the mysterious wise woman (a role she often plays in stories), and the reunion between Eagle and his wife is very moving. When the time comes for the spirits to drift back to their own land, George takes Belinda's hand for a moment and says, 'take care of yourself, dear'. The atmosphere at the end is very thoughtful and serene. I end by thanking everyone for the roles they have played and suggest a song. Quick as a wink, Edith suggests 'We'll meet again', which is a perfect choice. Several of the group know the words and the rest of us hum along.

The Crescent Moon Bear

Once there was a young woman whose husband was away for many years fighting a war. When he returned she was overjoyed to see him. She swept the house and made all manner of wonderful dishes for him. However, he was churlish and silent. He refused to enter the house and instead slept on stones outside. Every day he went into the forest and did not return for hours.

The young woman was dismayed. The more she tried to reach him the more he avoided her or pushed her away.

In desperation the young woman went to the cave of a healer who lived outside the village. She told him her story. He thought for a while and then said, 'I can help you cure your husband and return him to his old self but I am missing one vital ingredient which you will have to go and fetch for me'. The woman was delighted that the healer said he could help her: 'tell me what you need,' she said, 'it doesn't matter what it is, I shall fetch it for you'.

The healer said, 'I need a hair from the Crescent Moon Bear. Go to the mountain, find the bear and pluck a single hair from the crescent of white fur on its throat. Then I can return your husband to you as his old self'.

The woman thanked the healer profusely. She was not dismayed by the task for she was a woman who loved. She was so happy there was something that could be done for her husband.

She went home and packed a bag for her journey.

She set off and the journey to the foothills was relatively easy. Her heart sang as she journeyed. Soon she came to the mountain, which was surrounded by huge boulders which she had to clamber over. The stones were sharp and cut her hands and feet, but she was not downcast for she was a woman who loved.

She climbed all day until she could see the snow that lay on the mountain's peak. As dusk fell a wind blew up bringing stinging snow and ice. Still she climbed, for she was a woman who loved.

As she reached the peak of the mountain, night fell. She found herself a tiny cave in which to shelter. She didn't eat any of the food she had brought with her. She wrapped her shawl around herself and slept.

In the morning the air was crisp and cold and there was frost on the ground. She awoke feeling stiff and sore but eager to find the bear. She began to search and towards the end of the day came across the spoor of the bear. It wasn't long before she heard a roar and saw deep claw and pad marks in the snow. Across her path lumbered the huge black bear. He disappeared into his cave.

The woman knew what she must do. She took some of the food she had brought with her and placed it in a bowl in front of the cave. Then she ran and hid behind the trees and waited.

The bear smelt the delicious food and came warily out of its den. It smelt the air and the food suspiciously then gulped it in one gulp and disappeared back into its cave.

The next night, the woman did the same thing. This time she did not retreat into the trees as far. The bear came out for the food, roaring and sniffing the air. It gobbled the food and hastened back into its lair.

This continued for many nights, each night the woman moving a little closer to the cave until one night, when the bear lumbered out, the little woman was standing there.

The bear roared loud enough to wake the dead and reared up on its back legs pawing the air. The woman trembled so much she almost fell over but she stood her ground. 'Please, dear bear, it is I who have been feeding you these past nights, please can you give me a hair from your throat to cure my husband and return him to his old self?'

The bear looked at the woman who was standing before him. She would make an easy meal. But he was touched by her bravery and moved to pity.

'You may take one of my hairs, but only one and quickly and then you must return to your own.'

The bear lifted his chin so that the crescent-shaped fur was clearly visible. The woman could see a pulse beating strongly in his throat. She reached forward and quickly tugged out a hair. The bear roared and drew back.

'Oh, thank you, thank you,' said the woman as she took the precious hair and wrapped it in her clothes. She turned and fled back down the mountain as fast as she could. Without stopping to wash or feed herself, she went straight to the healer's cave and presented him with the hair.

'Here is the hair that you needed!' she cried.

The healer carefully took the hair and examined it. 'Yes,' he mused, 'this is indeed the hair of the Crescent Moon Bear'. Then he took it and cast it into the fire, where it burned to nothing in a second.

The woman wailed, 'what have you done?'.

'Do not be afraid,' said the healer, 'do you recall each step you took to scale the mountain, each step you took to earn the trust of the Crescent Moon Bear, everything you thought and felt and saw?'

'Yes,' said the woman, 'I remember it all very well.'

'Go,' said the healer, 'and with the same understanding proceed in the same way with your husband.'

The woman thanked the healer and made her way back home with hope in her heart that in time she could return her husband to her.

Themes in the story

You cannot work in elderly care without having some awareness of the impact the Second, and in some cases the First, World War had on your elderly clients. My theory is that these two events continue to have an enormous impact on all of us and that we haven't even begun to process these major global traumas.

In 1945 at the end of the war men came back from fighting and no provision was made to help them make the transition from war to peace time.

Some returned to children who didn't recognise them and changed domestic situations – a lot of wives waited for their husbands but some didn't. Some men had witnessed and experienced great atrocities of which they never spoke. The horrors that were unspoken but ever present created an enormous wedge in families. We know what happens to feelings when they are not expressed. They develop a charge around them which is an enemy to contact. This was the case in millions of families.

Post-traumatic stress syndrome was not a term used in those days – it was still the time of the stiff upper lip. We can see the effects of long-term post-traumatic stress in the lead up to the fiftieth anniversary celebrations of VE and VJ day in 1995. The Red Cross was inundated with requests for counselling for veterans who had had their memories painfully awakened fifty years after the event.

Not everyone's experience of the war was harrowing. My own father spoke of his youthful time in the army in Palestine with glowing nostalgia. In some ways, it was the most exciting and fulfilling period of his life. John Boorman's film *Hope and Glory* portrayed an idyllic childhood spent growing up during the war years. I think it is important to bear in mind that people had very varied experiences, so this is yet another occasion where the sensitive use of a story can be an appropriate approach because it leaves the individual room to identify with the characters or not.

Ostensibly the Japanese story, 'The Crescent Moon Bear', focuses on the experience of the wife, but who is the Crescent Moon Bear? He is the wild animal but also the traumatised husband. The image of the husband is very much of someone suffering post-traumatic stress. He is no longer at war but is having great difficulty adapting to his old life. He avoids contact with his wife and everyone else. He is very angry and takes out that anger on the person closest to him.

The story is explicit in the advice it gives on how to deal with someone in his position. A feature emphasised in the story is that the woman is not downcast at the difficulty of her task because she is glad to be able to do something. Such practical information is invaluable.

The healer in the story could have told the woman how best to approach her traumatised husband but instead he sets a task, the achievement of which gives her a felt, as well as a theoretical, understanding. We learn by doing.

On another level, this story is about the healing or transforming power of love. The nameless woman in the story is one of a long line of heroines who perform gruelling tasks in order to be reunited with their loved ones. Psyche in the Greek myths and Hans Christian Andersen's *Little Mermaid* are just two examples. In the end, the major task for the woman in this story is to be patient, not to try to rush things and little by little build up the trust of the other person. In this I think the story offers the most excellent advice to anyone wanting to work therapeutically with people.

Using the story in a session

I did this story with a youthful elderly group and it stimulated a huge amount of discussion.

One woman told me about her experience of being a child living in the East End during the war. The bombing got so bad that people were advised to go and stay with relatives outside London if they could. For so many people this was not possible as they didn't have relatives elsewhere. This woman was from a Jewish family whose ancestors had settled in the East End from Russia and Poland. Traditionally, Jews had gravitated towards the cities and not gone to rural areas. This woman's mother got so frightened that after listening to the radio one morning at breakfast she packed a bag for herself and her three children and left without a backward glance. At the train station they stood in a queue and asked the man in front where he was going. He said Bury St Edmunds so that's where they went. They turned up in Bury St Edmunds where they didn't know a soul and were looked after by the locals. There they spent the duration of the war. At the end of the war they returned to their house in Stepney after a three year absence to find everything just as they left it on that morning three years previously. The tea leaves were still in the pot waiting for the boiling water, the dishes set for breakfast.

This story always reminds me of the fairy tale of 'The Sleeping Beauty' where the prince discovers the overgrown palace that has been asleep for a hundred years. I have heard some people describe their experience of the war in these terms – that everything was put on hold for the duration of the war.

5

Loss of Home and Possessions

A theme of particular poignancy and importance to elderly people, and particularly those in a residential setting, is the theme of home.

I first used stories that looked at the theme of home when I was training as a drama therapist and I was running a group for adults who had been released into the community after many years in a psychiatric hospital. Ostensibly, this hospital had been a monstrosity, one of those Victorian horrors that people disappeared into for years on end. However, for members of this group it had been home for up to thirty years and there was huge anxiety as people struggled to make the transition into a totally different environment with very little support.

I was once asked to do a training session for the staff of a Housing Association which provided housing for people in need. They were often on the receiving end of verbal abuse and invective from the very people they were trying to help. We explored the symbol of home which gave people an insight into why it was such a charged issue. They began to see that 'home' is not just about people getting a roof over their heads.

The stories that I have chosen address the issue of loss of home from the point of view of what it's like to search for or create a home.

When I began to work in elderly care I was struck by what a major issue home was for the vast majority of people. I saw the efforts of staff to make the environment 'homely' and what a challenge that was. I was there when new residents came into care after they had had a stroke, knowing they would never return home again. I have seen people agonise over the decision of whether to place a much loved relative in a home. I have heard people calling out for their home: 'I want to go home' is a particularly heart rending thing to hear anyone cry, but particularly the older person for whom the return to their own home is unlikely.

The Water of Life

There once was a family of three brothers and a sister who decided to build a house.

They worked together for many years until they had built the most beautiful house and then they had a house warming and invited the whole village to come and see it.

The people walked around that house with their mouths ajar; it was so beautiful and perfect in every way.

However, there was one old woman who lived in the village who was not impressed. She told the family, 'There are three things missing from this house and they are the water of life, the flowering branch and the singing bird'. The family were dismayed as the old woman was very wise and they had no doubt that she spoke the truth.

'Grandmother,' said the sister very respectfully, 'what should we do?'

'The three things you need are at the top of yonder mountain,' said the old woman, 'and the only other help I can give you is to give you this.' She handed the sister a small knife: 'Watch the blade carefully and if ever it rusts you will know that one of you is in danger.'

With that the old woman disappeared into the crowd.

Immediately the elder brother cried: 'I shall be the one to go to the top of the mountain and find these three things. Take care of the house, all of you, until I return!'

So the brother set off on his journey. The way was long and arduous over rough, dry ground but within three days the brother came in sight of the mountain. What should he see at the foot of the mountain but a giant who guarded the way. 'Why have you come and what do you seek?' demanded the giant. 'I am seeking the water of life, the flowering branch and the singing bird so that I may make my house complete,' said the brother.

'What you seek is at the top of the mountain,' said the giant, 'and there is only one thing more I can tell you. As you ascend the mountain be careful to look neither to the right nor to the left and under no circumstances look behind you.' The brother thanked the giant for his advice and began his ascent. No sooner had he gone a few steps when he heard strange sounds and whisperings behind him and without thinking he turned his head and, pouf!, there he was turned into a shiny pebble on the side of the mountain.

Back home, his sister anxiously checked the knife to see if her brother was safe and that morning as she reached into the drawer she could see the blood red of rust upon the blade. Crying out, she called her brothers and showed them the knife. 'There's nothing for it,' said the middle brother, 'I must go and rescue our brother and bring back the water of life, the flowering branch and the singing bird.' And with that he set off with great speed across the rough ground.

Such was his haste that he made the journey in less than two days and arrived at the foot of the mountain just as the sun was setting. 'Why have you come and what do you seek?' demanded the giant from out of the shadows. 'I seek my brother, the water of life, the flowering branch and the singing bird. Can you help me?'

'This I can tell you,' said the giant 'Your brother has passed this way and the three things you seek are at the top of the mountain. But take care. As you ascend look neither to the right nor to the left and under no circumstances look behind you.' The brother thanked him and began his ascent of the mountain.

No sooner had he taken a step then he began to hear strange sounds and noises behind him. Resolutely he tried to close his ears against them but the voices became more and more insistent and when he heard his brother's voice calling him by name he turned to look without thinking. Immediately, pouf!, there he was, a stone lying on the lonely hillside.

Next morning his sister checked the knife as usual and gave out a little cry. Her brother came running and the two of them stared at the blade that was blood red with rust. 'There's nothing for it!' cried the younger brother, 'I must go and rescue my brothers and bring back the water of life, the flowering branch and the singing bird.'

With that he dashed off across the countryside towards the mountain and would have got there within a day had he not stopped when the darkness became too impenetrable for his eyes to see the ground before him.

First thing in the morning he got to the foot of the mountain and saw the giant before him. 'Why have you come and what do you seek?' demanded the giant.

'I come looking for my two brothers, the water of life, the flowering branch and the singing bird,' said the boy.

The giant replied, 'What you seek is up the mountain and I have one piece of advice to give you. As you ascend be careful to look neither to the right nor to the left and under no circumstances look behind you.' The boy thought to himself that this was an easy task to accomplish but he thanked the giant and eagerly strode up the mountain.

He had gone only a few steps when the voices started whispering. Bravely he tried to ignore them, even when he recognised the voices of his brothers calling him by name, but as their whisperings turned to taunts and then to jeers he could stand it no longer. He turned in fury and, pouf!, there he was, a boulder lying on the side of the mountain.

Sure enough, when the sister went to check the blade of the knife she found it red as blood with rust. Gathering up some things, she asked a neighbour to look after the house and set off towards the mountain.

It took her three days to reach the foot, where she met the giant who asked her what she had come for and gave her the advice: 'as you ascend look neither to the right nor to the left and under no circumstances look behind you.'

Scrambling up the mountain, for she was very tired and the way was hard, she began to hear voices and the voices of her three brothers calling her by name. She gritted her teeth and remembered the giant's advice and persevered. On and on she climbed with the voices getting louder and more persistent, but still she persisted looking neither to the right nor to the left and never, ever, looking behind her.

All at once she reached the top of the mountain and there to her amazement she saw a brook bubbling up with water overhung by a flowering tree with a magnificent bird singing in its branches. Taking a jug out of her bag, she filled it with water, plucked a branch from the tree and the bird flew and settled itself on the branch.

Then she began to make her way back down the mountain. But the way was very rocky and her arms were full and as she went she slipped and splashed some of the water from the jug on the stony ground and behold up leapt young men and women. And realising what had happened she emptied the jug on the ground and went back to the brook to get more, and stone after stone materialised into a person long imprisoned on the windy hillside.

Finally there were her own dear brothers who were overjoyed and embraced her and danced her around while the mountain continued to surrender up its secret population of people petrified in stone.

Together everyone made their way back down the mountain where they had a celebration and thanked the sister for releasing them. Then they made their separate ways back home – the three brothers and the sister back to their lovely house.

When they arrived they poured the water of life into a fountain in the garden, planted the branch beside it and the singing bird flew up into its branches. At last the house had become a home.

And they all lived happily ever after.

Themes in the story

The quest at the centre of this Catalan story is reminiscent of Psyche's tasks in the Greek myth of Psyche and Amor in that it requires real concentration and focus not to get distracted or even to respond to the voices of loved ones.

It is interesting that it is the sister who achieves what the brothers cannot. Often that single-minded refusal to get distracted is associated with a masculine approach whereas women are seen as being able to respond to a number of requests and juggle differing needs at one time but find it more difficult to focus on one thing, and find it particularly difficult to ignore requests for help. Certainly this is Robert Johnson's interpretation of the nature of Psyche's tasks, that Psyche needs to develop the more masculine side of her personality in order to achieve the tasks set her by Aphrodite to win back her lover, Amor.[1]

The image of the people turned into stone is an interesting one, and often occurs in stories (see `Maple Leaf Devil', where the heroine is turned into a statue). It is an image of something petrified and unchanging which can have both positive and negative associations. There is an old Welsh myth about a man stumbling on an underground passage that leads to a room that is full of knights of the Round Table and King Arthur, slumbering until the time of England's greatest need when they will re-awaken. This is an image of stasis where energy is conserved until it's really needed.

The water of life revives the people imprisoned in stone. Water is generally associated with emotions in Jungian terms, but it can have many meanings and is a wonderful symbol to work with.

Using the story in a session

In one session where I used this story with a group with dementia, the woman playing the sister spontaneously cupped her hands and offered 'water' to other people in the group. As the narrator I reminded them, 'in the story the water of life revives and refreshes the people imprisoned in stone'. I was amazed at how 'thirsty' people were. Some people mimed drinking the water from Dolly's hands for what seemed like ages.

On another level, water symbolises fluidity and flexibility and is in stark contrast to the stones, which are fixed and immobile. What I stress in working with people is flexibility and being able to flow with a group and not to have too rigid a view of what a session should look like.

In groups I ask the question, 'what makes a house into a home?'. People's answers are very illuminating. One woman (who fortunately had her cat with her in the nursing home) said pets make a house homely. One man said an open fire. A lot of people said family and friends.

In one group I told them that the story was to be about a family designing and building their home and asked if they were going to do that which room would be the most important to them. People seemed to really enjoy thinking and talking about this. One woman said the library would be the

---

1   Robert Johnson (1989) *She*. Perenial.

most important, one woman said the conservatory. One man said a room where he could sit and listen to music.

Maple Leaf Devil

Once there was a couple who married against their parents' wishes and so had to flee the place where they grew up.

In the course of their travels they came upon a mountain that they had to cross in order to continue their journey. It was a very beautiful wooded mountain but as they climbed they were struck by the almost supernatural stillness. Not a leaf stirred nor a bird called.

As they toiled on the young man, whose name was Chang, grew more and more uneasy. He urged his young wife to hurry as he really wanted to put the mountain behind them.

Suddenly they came upon a pond of clear water and before Chang could remonstrate his young wife had bent down to drink the water greedily. As she lifted her face to her husband he saw a subtle transformation. Where before she had been looking pale and thin, her face was now pink and plump.

'Drink, husband. This water is so reviving,' she said.

But he would have none of it. He pulled his wife to her feet and insisted they continue on their journey. He had such a strong sense of foreboding he almost ran down the mountain on to the plains below.

That night they stopped in a little village and were given food and shelter by an old woman who lived alone.

As they were drinking tea the young woman, Gong Li, told the woman about the wonderful water that had so revived her.

'Aiee!' said the old woman, 'any woman who drinks from the pool of Maple Leaf Devil becomes his bride and at autumn he comes to claim them.'

The old woman got so upset they had to calm her. Chang pretended it was an old wives tale but in his heart he was troubled.

Next day, the old woman made them a proposition. She said, 'why don't you settle here and help me on the land? There is room enough for all of us and you can inherit the land when I am gone'.

The couple agreed and the three began to live happily together.

The summer passed while they worked the fields, and Chang and Gong Li forgot about Maple Leaf Devil. The old woman didn't forget, however. Every night she clutched her quilt around her and listened for the first of the autumn winds with dread.

Time passed and summer gave way to autumn.

One night there was a huge full moon. Gong Li called Chang and the old woman to her to look. As they gazed up in wonder they saw there was something outlined against the white of the moon. What was it? Could it be a bird or a bat, maybe? As it got closer they could see it was a furled up maple leaf and as it hit the ground up sprang Maple Leaf Devil.

He was huge with blood red eyes, mahogany skin and a magnificent oiled moustache that curled up at both ends.

'I am Maple Leaf Devil!' he cried, 'and I have come to claim my bride!'

With that he scooped up Gong Li and disappeared.

Immediately the old woman began to rend her clothes and pull her hair and cry, but Chang put his best foot forward and set out towards Maple Leaf mountain to rescue his bride.

In the middle of the mountain, Maple Leaf Devil had very luxurious apartments, where he was trying to seduce Gong Li. She, however, would not stop crying and calling for her husband. Maple Leaf Devil poured her some wine and played soft music, to little effect. Suddenly his red eyes bored through the mountain and he saw Chang making his way across the plain.

Maple Leaf Devil was furious. He threw down his wine and immediately Chang was faced by a rushing torrential river that appeared out of nowhere. Undaunted he waded in and swam to the other side.

Maple Leaf Devil tried whispering sweet nothings in the pearly little ear of Gong Li but she sobbed even more. Suddenly his red eyes saw that Chang was still advancing and now making his way up the mountain.

Maple Leaf Devil drew off the belt of his robe and threw it on the ground. It immediately turned into a fearsome tiger that raced down the mountain and leapt on to Chang, savaging him to the ground.

Maple Leaf Devil returned to Gong Li, who still wouldn't stop crying. He started to lose patience, especially when he saw that Chang had despatched the tiger and transformed it back into a harmless length of cloth. He was now making his way into the apartments of Maple Leaf Devil.

Maple Leaf Devil had never encountered such resistance and determination before. He decided that if he couldn't have Gong Li nobody could. In a flash he turned her into a statue and disappeared.

Chang came running into the apartments of Maple Leaf Devil and what should he find but his beloved, cold and insensible. He watched a single tear run down the alabaster cheek.

Sobbing, he decided to take the statue back to his home and the old woman. He hoisted it on to his back and began to make his weary way down the mountain.

Suddenly his path was blocked by none other than Maple Leaf Devil. He was shocked to hear a repentant Maple Leaf Devil say, 'I have loved many women but never as you love Gong Li. It makes me ashamed that I prey on young women and I vow never to do it again'.

With that he disappeared in a flurry of maple leaves and Chang found himself carrying the warm, living body of his dear wife.

The couple hugged each other delightedly and then made their way back home to the old woman, who was overjoyed to see them.

And they all lived happily ever after.

Themes in the story

I could easily have included this Chinese story in the chapters on loss of a person (Chang loses and regains his beloved Gong Li), positive elderly figures (the old woman who offers them a home and a future) or marriage and the joy of union (the couple strive to be together through many obstacles and the steadfastness of their love transforms the devil). The best stories are multi-layered and as the facilitator we can choose which aspect to focus on in the session. This is the richness of working with stories.

Some people may have had experience of or known couples who have lost contact with their families because of their choice of partner. This could involve being actively ostracised or having to move to be near the husband or the husband's work.

I think it is tremendously positive that it is a lonely old woman who offers the couple a home in a mutually beneficial arrangement.

Unlike the previous story, here we have an image of water that is reviving but potentially very dangerous. It reminds me of Persephone eating the pomegranate seeds that bind her in some way to the underworld. Maple Leaf Devil is a very different figure to Hades, but he claims ownership on the basis of water consumed on his territory.

Using the story in a session

I have had great fun with this story and it contains much that an older group can enjoy. The character of Maple Leaf Devil is amusing. One group I had included a man who was blind and extremely flirtatious. One of the objects I had brought in was an extremely ornate brocade dressing gown which I thought looked Chinese. In the enactment Jim wore this and became very debonair. He was clean shaven but mimed twirling his moustache 'devilishly'.

It was this story that taught me some of the benefits of having action elements in a story. I used this in the very early days of a group who were all in wheelchairs and whose energy was often really low. I discovered one way to get people to sit up and take notice was to provide pieces of action that were loud and rambunctious. As I hadn't been working with this group for very long I asked a young male nurse to be the rushing river and fierce tiger that Maple Leaf Devil sends to despatch Chang. My co-leader was playing Chang and she was wrestled to the ground by a very enthusiastic 'river' and 'tiger' with much shrieking and shouting. The group were absolutely riveted and laughed a lot. I watched closely to see if anyone looked alarmed but everyone seemed to realise 'it was in the story'.

The Bird of Happiness

There was once a young boy called Aaron who lived with his parents in the desert. They had no home and very few possessions, for his parents had been slaves, and every day they had to search for food and water. It was a hard life and they were constantly exposed to the elements but Aaron's father always said, 'some day the Bird of Happiness will guide us to Jerusalem'.

And so they travelled through the desert for many years.

One night Aaron had a vivid dream. He dreamt a sand storm blew up. Everything grew dark and the family crouched beneath their cloaks waiting for it to blow over. When it did they found they were hopelessly lost. Just when they had given up hope of ever finding their way, Aaron saw a speck on the horizon. As it came nearer he saw it was a beautiful white bird. It flew above his head, opened its beak and dropped something into his outstretched hand.

Aaron awoke with a start to find he was holding in his hand a glowing stone. He showed it to his mother and told her his dream and she said, 'the stone is a gift from the Bird of Happiness. We are blessed'.

Aaron fastened a strip of leather to the stone and hung it around his neck with the stone resting on his heart.

He discovered the stone was an invaluable guide for it glowed when they were going in the direction of food and water and dimmed when they were not. In this way they discovered every fragrant oasis dripping with fruit the desert could offer up.

After years they came to a walled city. Aaron's eyes were like saucers as he had lived his whole life in the desert and never seen anything like this city teeming with people.

Aaron's father asked a man what city it was and he told them it was Jerusalem and there was great consternation because the king had just died and the people were waiting for the arrival of the Bird of Happiness to choose his successor.

Aaron looked up to the sky eagerly. He couldn't believe he was in the magical city *and* about to see the Bird of Happiness.

Soon there was a flurry of excitement and high above them flew a beautiful white bird. Aaron recognised it as the bird of his dream. The bird circled over the city and then began to descend. Down and down it flew until it settled right on top of Aaron's head. A great cheer went up from the crowd, 'hail to our new king!', and Aaron and his parents were ushered to the magnificent palace in the centre of the city.

So Aaron became king and was crowned with all proper pomp and ceremony. He lived in the palace with his parents and ruled wisely, guided by the stone that glowed brightly to signify yes and dully to signify no. And he never again had to sleep on sand or endure the harsh light of the sun.

Themes in the story

On one level the story is very clearly the story of a family's search for a home. On another level it is the story of the Jewish people or any displaced or exiled people trying to find somewhere of their own to settle.

The wandering life is full of hardship but the family is sustained by the faith of the father who reiterates, 'some day the Bird of Happiness will guide us to Jerusalem'. Great hardships can be endured with faith and a vision of the future.

The motif of the guiding dream is an important one which is common in stories.

The dream is a symbol of the unconscious which contains information unknown by the conscious mind that can transform the waking life. The stone is a symbol of this intuitive knowing present in the dream and transformed into a concrete object when Aaron awakes. The stone is the guiding power of the unconscious that has wisdom that cannot be accessed by will alone. The story is saying that we can wander in the desert which is dry, barren and cannot sustain us and easily lose direction without the guiding power of the unconscious.

Life is improved once Aaron connects with this part of himself and allows himself to be influenced by it and to be led by it where he needs to go. It leads him to lush, fertile places and eventually the realisation of his potential. He is ready not only to find his kingdom but to rule his kingdom. In other words he assumes responsibility and authority in his own life.

The 'Hymn of the pearl' is a classic story of taking one's place as ruler in one's own kingdom; in other words being in charge of one's own life on every level, not just literally but also spiritually and psychologically. In that story the central character is the son of a king and a queen but has to put off his royal robes in order to 'go down into Egypt' to claim a pearl from the coils of a serpent deep within a lake. Basically it is saying we have to strive to claim what is ours by birth but cannot be bequeathed by our parents, in other words, our parents cannot do it for us.

The story makes a very deep connection between a literal home made out of bricks and mortar and the home as a symbol of the self. The person who has undergone this journey of maturation is 'at home in himself', which is indeed an achievement.

Using the story in a session

I did this story with a group who I had worked with for about six months before I took a long summer break.

The group were all in wheelchairs apart from one man, and I had two regular supporters who made the work pleasurable and easy. One of the residents loved the stories and was very wise to the underlying aims. She said to me once after a session, 'you're so clever, aren't you? You tell us a lovely story and get us to do all these things and we don't even realise we're doing them'.

One of the men who supported me was a particular favourite of this woman's. He was a man in his fifties who had been a nurse but health problems forced him to take early retirement. He got very bored at home but was restricted by his health from doing very much. The sessions offered him the opportunity to be in a familiar environment and helping role without putting too many demands on him.

As this was the last session for six weeks I wanted to leave something with people that they could keep. I toyed with the idea of bringing in fresh flowers to use as objects and linking them with the story by talking about deserts and oases, but I knew that they wouldn't keep for more than a week. Instead I brought in a selection of pebbles and semi-precious stones which people could look at and hold and keep. As long as they were very clean, stones and pebbles always proved to be very popular with groups. People seemed to like to hold them in their hands. (The only group I learnt to be a bit careful with was dementia groups where a feature of the disease can be hyper orality – a tendency to put objects in the mouth, in some ways mirroring the behaviour of infants, whose major sense for experiencing the world is taste. I used to like involving people in my life so when I returned from holiday I would often include as objects things from my vacation. One time I brought a box of small shells to show a dementia group, explaining I had been in Greece and my husband had gone snorkelling and fished these shells up from the bottom of the ocean. I had been engrossed in conversation with someone when I turned around and was appalled to find one woman had put a tiny sea anemone shell in her mouth and was thoughtfully crunching it up. Fortunately she suffered no harm and didn't even seem to object to the taste, but I was very vigilant with small 'bite sized' objects from then on.)

The stones' link with the story was, of course, the magical stone that guides the boy.

The other object I used was halva. Halva is a Middle Eastern sweetmeat made out of sesame seed. I brought it because it was rare to use an object that appealed to the sense of taste. Halva is very, very sweet and sticky – probably not ideal for false teeth but it stimulated lots of different reactions!

In the story Anne played Aaron and she wanted Jim to be the Bird of Happiness. Nancy, who was a lady with dementia who could be very lucid, asked to be an oasis, which was a role I hadn't even thought of. Michael, who was mobile and unsighted, and Lily, in a wheelchair, played Aaron's parents. This worked well as Barry and I could push two chairs around accompanied by Michael to convey the arduous journey. Michael was very convincing as he complained all the time about how tired he was. When the stone guided the family to the oasis I said of Nancy in her role as the oasis, 'see, this beautiful, abundant place rimmed with palm trees'. Nancy then lifted up her arms and said, 'come, come'. Michael said, 'we are very thirsty and tired' and Nancy said, 'come and have a nice cup of tea'.

We had a new lady that week who would become one of the most active members of the group; her name was Emma. She had opted to play one of the city dwellers in Jerusalem but when it came to the part where Aaron and his parents arrive and ask where they are and what is happening, she took the initiative and became the spokesperson. I was amazed at how much she remembered from one telling of the story. I hardly had to prompt her at all. When Aaron became king I took liberties with the story and said that he chose Emma as his chief counsel as she was so wise.

To focus on loss of possessions is one way to approach issues such as bereavement in an even more indirect way, but the loss of possessions is an issue in itself and very relevant to an elderly group.

Staff sometimes find it hard to understand why someone who is very disabled and finding looking after themselves very difficult should fight to stay in their own home with all their own things around them. With the current health policies of care in the community, people are going to be staying in their own homes for as long as possible. However, eventually for some people a move into residential care becomes the only option.

In training, I use a very simple exercise to help people understand the significance and importance of certain possessions to them.

I ask people to think of the size of the average fruit or beer crate. I ask them, 'what if you had to go somewhere and could only take the belongings that fit in that crate? What would you take and what would you leave behind?'. I tell them to make a list.

The size of the crate corresponds to the size of the average bedside cabinet, which is often all people in a residential home or hospital have for their exclusive use.

In some cases, for example if someone suddenly becomes incapacitated either through a stroke or a sudden worsening of a dementing illness and they have to be taken into care, someone other than themselves is given the responsibility of going to their home and choosing what belongings can come with them into the home. Can you imagine someone else having to decide out of all your things what is important to you and what isn't? How would you feel about that?

This is a theoretical exercise but it can provide loads of interesting information. Here are some of the choices people in my training groups made.

Many people opted to take a travel kettle in their box so they could make a cup of tea when they felt like it. This gave a real appreciation of how difficult it must be to live in a home where you cannot get up and make a cup of tea when you want. I had one woman say, 'I get so irritated when Mabel keeps asking for a cup of tea, now I understand it more. Tea time is a major event in residential homes and hospitals, and staff often don't understand the significance of it or why some residents constantly ask for tea (aside from the purely practical reasons of overheated homes and/or medication making people very thirsty).

Very often people will include practical items such as passport, cheque book and birth certificate that relate very much to issues of autonomy, freedom and identity.

Another common feature is the presence of items relating to personal hygiene: toothbrushes, flannels, soap. One woman said that as her residents suffered memory loss she was not that concerned about washing people with their own things as 'they would never know'. She revised her opinion when she realised how important these personal items were to her and how much she would hate being washed with someone else's flannel, for example.

It is also interesting to see what we choose to leave behind or what cannot be fitted in the box. The box would not allow for pets or other living things such as plants. Very few residential homes enable a person to bring a pet and separation from them can be extremely distressing.

The Widow and the Honey Pots

There was once a young widow who lived in Israel at a time when it was ruled by Syria. The captain of the town wished to marry her as she was very fair and besides had plenty of money, and he made his feelings known.

The young woman had no desire to marry the man but was afraid to make an enemy of him as he was very powerful. She decided to leave and go and visit her sister in another part of the country and hope that the captain would in the meantime transfer his affections to someone else.

So she summoned her maid to her and told her to pack what they would need for a long journey. Meanwhile the widow pondered the safest place for all the gold coins she owned that her husband had left her. She knew it would be unwise to take them with her, but where could she leave them where no one could discover them?

Suddenly she had an idea. Down in the cellar there were large pitchers which were used for storage. She could hide the money in them. She and her maid went down to the cellar where they put the gold coins in the jars and then sealed the top with a thick layer of honey. The money suitably disguised, she then went and asked her neighbours if they minded looking after her honey pots until her return. The neighbours were more than happy to and they transferred the pots to the neighbours' cellar. Then the widow and her maid set off with easy hearts.

Now after a time, one of the neighbours' sons married and at the wedding feast they ran out of sweetmeats for the guests. Suddenly the father remembered the widow's honey and decided to take some, with the intention of replacing it afterwards. Imagine his surprise when scraping back a layer of the sticky honey he saw the glint of gold. Quickly he emptied all the jars and there was the widow's treasure. Unable to resist the temptation, he and his family took the gold and filled up the jars again with honey.

Some weeks later, news came to the widow that the Syrian captain had received promotion and had been transferred to another town. Excitedly she made preparations to return home.

Of course, as soon as she returned the first thing she did was to send her maid to fetch the honey pots from her neighbours. When they were safely back in her own cellar she eagerly began to scrape back the honey to find…more honey! The pots were entirely full of honey. The treasure had gone.

Frantically the widow went to her neighbours and demanded to know where her gold was. Coolly they denied everything. All they knew was that they had been entrusted with pots of honey. Had she not got them back safely?

There began for the widow a desperate quest for justice.

She took her case to the judges, who asked her, 'did anyone see you put the coins in the jars?'. 'Only my maid', replied the widow. 'Ah well, you have no witnesses, so it is only your word against theirs. We cannot help you.'

Eventually she went to the court of King Saul and managed to get an audience with him. However, the king asked the same question: 'do you have any witnesses who can vouch for what you say?'. The widow sadly shook her head. 'Well I'm afraid there is nothing I or anyone can do for you.'

The widow was weeping as she left the court when she was approached by a young boy who said to her, 'I overheard your case and I think I might be able to help you. Will you let me speak for you?'. The widow eagerly agreed and permission was granted from the judges.

The boy called all the people involved in the case together, including the judges. 'It seems that what is lacking in this case is witnesses,' said the boy. 'If you would accompany me to the house of the widow I will produce some witnesses for you.'

Intrigued, the people made their way to the widow's house and down into the cellar where the honey pots were. 'Are these the pots?' asked the boy. The widow nodded. 'Are these the pots you safeguarded for the widow?' the boy asked the neighbours. The neighbours nodded. With that the boy took a hammer and smashed all the pots to pieces. As everyone was recovering from the shock he bent down and retrieved from the floor a shard from the bottom of a pot. There glistening and stuck with honey were two gold coins. The boy held them aloft. 'Here are your silent witnesses.'

With that the neighbours broke down and confessed their dishonesty and agreed to return the widow's money and more besides. The widow thanked the boy profusely. 'How can I repay your kindness? You helped me when no one else would and your ingenuity has returned what was stolen from me.' The boy shook his head. 'I want no reward. It is enough that justice has been done.' And with that they all lived happily ever after.

Themes in the story

The story is a Jewish folk tale with no magical elements, very much in the tradition of a story concerned with having a comfortable life, enough funds and finding a suitable partner – although in this case it's more about avoiding an unsuitable one!

The original Jewish story identifies the boy at the end of the story as the young David, who eventually becomes king. With groups that may have no knowledge of key figures in Jewish history I usually use the version above.

The major obvious loss in the story is the gold in the honey pots. It has only been through working a lot with elderly people that I appreciate how much distrust there is of banks and that the joke of hiding money under the mattress is not such a joke. The Depression of the 1930s was initiated by the Wall Street Crash, which some people still remember. I have had a lot of people identify with the widow's dilemma of how she could safeguard her money.

On another level the story involves a loss of trust – the widow loses trust in her neighbours and also the authorities, who are powerless to help her. When I used this story with a group in a day centre they were all living in their own homes, often alone. There were many stories of muggings and break-ins that people seemed to need to talk about. They lived in an area of the East End of London that had been a very stable community in the past but which they had seen change a lot over the years. They didn't feel they could trust their neighbours and they looked back at a time when they felt that they could with nostalgia and sadness.

The woman is portrayed as vulnerable despite all her money and a lot of people have identified with that aspect of her situation.

The story encourages us to ask the question: 'if I were in this situation, who would speak up for me, who would be my advocate?' and the authorities we would expect to support the widow let her down. This mirrors the experience of a lot of elderly people living independently. I have heard many older people complain that their GP hasn't time for them any more. Nowadays, people tend to have a much more remote relationship with the police in urban areas, but some people have spoken about the time when they used to know their 'bobby on the beat' by name. In this story help comes from an unlikely quarter, a young boy.

It is very common for residents in a home to complain that someone is stealing their things. This can be very distressing for staff. In training I approach it from several angles. One is to check out the veracity of the statement. It is always possible for things to get lost or mislaid as well as stolen. The other is to see the person in the residential home as a person who has lost a lot and if they are dementing they are in the process of losing even more. On an emotional level, the accusations of theft (as long as they are unfounded) can be an expression of this.

The Shining Fish

Once there was an old couple whose sons had died who were finding it very difficult to manage as they were very poor and the wife was ailing.

One day as he was making his way through the wood the old man met a gentleman who said to him, 'I know who you are and how much of a struggle your life is. Here's 1000 ducats in a silk purse'. The old man was so shocked that he fainted but when he came to the gentleman was gone and there lying beside him was the silk purse filled with gold.

The old man went home but didn't tell his wife of their good fortune for he feared her extravagance. Instead he hid the purse in a pile of manure and the next day went off to the woods as usual.

When he came home he found the table full of food. 'How did you manage to buy all this?' he asked in amazement. 'I sold the manure and with the money I was able to buy some food,' his wife replied innocently. The old man groaned inwardly but said nothing.

The next day he went off to the woods in a deep depression. There he came upon the same gentleman who said to him, 'don't look so glum. I know what happened. Here is another 1000 ducats'.

The old man was overjoyed and hid the ducats in the woodpile and went into his wife as if nothing had happened.

Next day he went off to the woods as usual but when he returned home he found his wife waiting with a handsome supper. 'Where did you get the money for all this?' he asked her with some trepidation. 'I sold wood from the woodpile,' she replied and the old man buried his head in his hands but he told her nothing.

The next day he went off to the woods weeping and came upon the gentleman who said to him, 'do not grieve. Take these twenty-four frogs and sell them to buy the biggest fish you can find'. The man obeyed. He went to market, sold the frogs and bought the biggest fish, which he took home with him.

That night the couple hung the fish outside to keep it fresh.

As darkness fell the fish began to glow and then to shine. It was a stormy night and out at sea the fishermen were having difficulty steering back to land. Suddenly one saw a light from the shore and steered towards it. As they got closer they saw it was the light from an enormous fish hanging outside a house. The fishermen successfully anchored and they made their way to the old man's house. They thanked him for providing such a beacon and gave him half their catch of fish. They made an agreement to share their catch with him in return for hanging up the fish every night.

The money they made from the catch meant the old man and his wife never went without again.

Themes in the story

This is an Italian story which I have used with a variety of groups. It is a very intriguing story. Who is the mysterious man in the forest? We never get to find out. Why twenty-four frogs? It's quite a mysterious landscape that's painted and one where anything can happen.

The most obvious feature is that they are an elderly couple who are very poor. There are going to be a lot of people who identify with that. Very often people suffer a marked loss in income as they get older.

It is another feature of the story that the old man is very secretive with money and that proves to be his downfall. I've had really interesting discussions with people around how finances were organised in their family. So many women told me, 'I never knew how much my husband earned, he would give me my housekeeping and that was it'. I would ask people if they thought women were extravagant, in other words was the old man right to conceal his good fortune from his wife for fear that she would squander the lot? Some people thought that women on the whole were extravagant and that they did like to spend money whereas some people thought that women were much better with money than men.

On another level, there is something very mean about someone who doesn't share his good fortune with his nearest and dearest. How does he hide his excitement from his wife? He hides his good fortune, he doesn't want to share even the fact of having it and so he loses it.

The fish shines. It won't be hidden. It attracts others to it. The fear of attracting attention to his new wealth may have been behind the old man's secretive behaviour. You often hear of lottery winners wanting to remain anonymous in case they get inundated by begging letters. What this means, however, is that they cannot enjoy their good fortune. They act as if they are still poor even when the reality belies that.

The character of the gentleman in the forest is important as he is very affirming, 'I can see how hard your life is' and supportive, 'I am going to help you'. He's also very patient. He does not berate the old man for not hanging on to the money. After two attempts with money he tries a slightly different tack by offering the frogs and some quite simple instructions. In these ways he offers a very good model of behaviour towards an older person.

How the Villagers found Wisdom

There was once a village set beside the sea in Yugoslavia.

All had enough to eat, no obvious hardship was endured, but as time went on there was a growing unease. People would gather to discuss 'what is missing in our village?'.

One day someone thought they had the answer: 'I know what we are missing here! We don't have enough wisdom'.

Well you know what it's like when someone plants an idea, it just grows until it seems really obvious to everyone 'what we need round here is more wisdom'. After initially being excited that they had pinpointed the problem the people became despondent once more: 'if, as you say, we need more wisdom, where are we to find it?'. This stimulated more discussion, with various people putting forward ideas on where to find wisdom.

Suddenly a man came forward and announced, 'I know where we can find wisdom. Venice is renowned for its wisdom. Surely we can buy some there'.

The people seized on this as a brilliant idea and soon were organising a group to sail across the sea to Venice to find some wisdom. One person was responsible for gathering as much gold and silver from people as they could afford because no one had any idea how much wisdom would cost. Soon everyone was congregated on the harbour to cheer and wave off the team who were entrusted with the task. A fair wind blew and off they went to Venice.

When they got within sight of Venice they were full of awe at the stunning buildings and glittering spires. 'Here indeed must wisdom reside,' they thought.

They then began to go through the city asking people where they could find wisdom. Reactions to their quest were mixed. Some people laughed at them, some people looked angry. They wandered all day through the city without any luck.

They came to the attention of a wily Venetian who saw a way of separating them from their money. He allowed himself to be approached by them and when asked, 'do you know where we can buy any wisdom?' replied, 'Yes, indeed I do'. The villagers were overjoyed and enquired eagerly of the man. He told them to return the following day to this same square and bring their money with them and he would bring the wisdom.

The Venetian went home and trapped a tiny mouse in a box and returned the following day to the square. 'Here is the wisdom, now where is your money?' he asked.

The villagers eagerly handed over all the money they had, although they were a bit dismayed at the size of the box. One of them immediately began to open the box but the Venetian stopped him. 'You must on no account open the box until you reach your own shores, otherwise the power of the wisdom will be destroyed. Do you give me your word?' The villagers agreed and the Venetian took their money and disappeared.

Sailing home the villagers were in high spirits, having achieved their aim. They talked about what heroes they would be when they returned to the village.

However, one or two began to get a bit restless and curious to see what wisdom looked like. One said, 'Surely we are entitled to take some for ourselves as we have had the hardship of making this journey and trailing around Venice searching'. Some reminded him of their promise to the Venetian but interest in seeing inside the box grew until eventually they all gathered in the hold of the ship to open the box.

Gathered in the semi-darkness one gingerly opened the box and screamed as a flash of white escaped from the box and disappeared into the shadowy depths of the ship. 'Oh, no, the wisdom is lost!' they cried as they searched on their hands and knees in the gloomy darkness.

Suddenly a cry came from above: land had been sighted. As they came within sight of their homeland they searched frantically throughout the ship to no avail.

On the shore their fellow villagers waited expectantly. They called out, 'did you get the wisdom?'. 'Yes', they replied. A cheer went up from the crowd. 'The only thing is, we've lost it.' The crowd groaned.

As the ship drew into the harbour the crew told their story. Everyone stood looking shocked and horrified. Suddenly someone had an idea: 'isn't the wisdom somewhere on the ship?'. The crew agreed that it was. 'Well, why don't we pull the ship up on to dry land and post a sentry on it and when we need some wisdom we can go and sit in the ship'. The others agreed this was a splendid idea and the whole village helped to pull the boat up on to the shore and take it in turns to stand guard.

From then on whenever anyone had a problem or something on their mind they would go and sit in the boat beside the shore to absorb some wisdom. And do you know, it never failed. Sometimes it took an hour, sometimes but a few moments, but no one went away without the wisdom they craved, and this is how the villagers bought wisdom.

Themes in the story

This story contains much that is relevant and affirming for an elderly group. It is one that I have often used with a new group. There are no named characters but plenty of opportunities to play a role within a group.

I have used this story with a dementia group and while I think that the complex idea that it plays around with, that is, what is concrete and what is a concept, may have been missed by some people there is much else in the story for them to enjoy.

There is much that is fruitful in the themes of what is wisdom and where we find it. I have had many responses to this question. Some people have said you can get wisdom from books, some that you are born with it, some that you can learn it in school. Many, many people have said that you only acquire wisdom through life experience and that you get wiser as you get older.

A lot of people have been conned at some time in their lives and elderly people are particularly vulnerable.

Loss is a major theme in the story because it begins with the people experiencing a growing sense of loss. Once they have identified the nature of the loss they then set about trying to rectify it. And what energy they use to do this! They organise a whip round, they mobilise a party of people to go do it, they set sail, get to Venice successfully and immediately scour the city for sources of wisdom. They are extremely resourceful. I do not see them being presented as country bumpkins or fools, merely as very unworldly and unsophisticated. It is interesting also that the story's resolution enables them to retain their naiveté, so the attitude of the story towards naivet, is not negative or it would disabuse them of it but it doesn't. We can smile at the image of these people projecting their own inner wisdom on to something as ridiculous as a small white mouse but we do that all the time. How many of us if we just took the time to tune in to ourselves would have all the answers to our problems.

The villagers at the beginning of the story are not in touch with their wisdom. There are similarities with the story of Aaron and the Bird of Happiness. There is a genuine lack at that time that is not imaginary. It is the journey, the struggle, the questing and questioning that serve to activate the quality they have already combined with a quiet, calm, conducive environment, namely the ship beached on the sea shore.

The story deals really well with a pattern of losing and finding and all the feelings associated with this. When the villagers buy the 'wisdom' from the Venetian they are jubilant and when they lose it on the ship they are very despondent. This theme is repeated again with the villagers on the shore. When they are told the wisdom has been found they respond with great gladness, followed by disappointment when they discover its loss.

Again, the story ends with a workable compromise and resolution. It is one the villagers can all live with. It's not perfect but it works.

Using the story in a session

I have often used limbers with a nautical theme for this story with the pulling up of sails and the scrubbing of decks.

The types of object that have gone down really well and have been very stimulating for people have been different examples of boxes. I have asked, 'what would you put in this box? What do you think it's made of? Where do you think it's come from?'.

The story is set by the sea so you could use wonderful things with a sea theme: shells, conches, seaweed, long swathes of sea blue material.

Because there are no named characters in the story I have often got a lot of people involved in taking part by playing one of the villagers. How I do that is to ask people if they want to be one of the villagers who go on the quest or those who stay to keep the home fires burning. 'Keep the home fires burning' is a phrase I use deliberately as it's familiar to people from the Second World War and it affirms the importance of this role. We can't all be adventurers – we need people to keep the spirit of the community alive and attend to other concerns such as bringing up children. What I try to emphasise is the importance of the part everyone plays in the life of the group. So even if someone declines to take a role, I thank them at the end for being part of the audience.

The wily Venetian is a very popular role. There is almost always someone who loves playing the 'con man'.

I am always interested whenever there is a debate about expunging characters that are thought of as 'negative' out of traditional stories for various reasons. Some people have rewritten fairy stories for children, making them less violent and bloodthirsty despite the fact that it is often these features that make them attractive to children.[2] It is no coincidence that the favourite modern children's story writer is Roald Dahl, who writes stories that are full of 'nasty' characters which children adore.

This debate ignores the psychological implications of stories, which on a very deep level are describing the different and sometimes contradictory parts of a whole person and present an image of wholeness. Jung referred to the 'shadow' as a part of the self the person refuses to acknowledge. The more the person does this the more powerful it becomes because it is operating outside the realms of their awareness and therefore is potentially dangerous. The shadow part is whatever is not owned so it could be a person's sadness or guilt. Often, though, it is the parts that are considered unacceptable by society – our 'nasty' parts. Certain characters in stories personify these aspects of the shadow and people often display great relish and excitement in acting them out. The wily Venetian is one such part.

2   Bruno Bettleheim (1976) *The Uses of Enchantment.* London: Penguin.

6

The Theme of Marriage
and the Joy of Union

This is an incredibly fruitful theme for discussion and exploration with a group or individual. In my experience I have found a fascination with this theme which transcends or contrasts with the person's own experience of marriage.

In a very youthful Jewish group I worked with, a number of the women had had matches made with someone they didn't know and the ensuing marriage had been very difficult. One woman told me, 'I hardly knew my husband when we got married and the first few years were awful. I used to cry myself to sleep every night'. Some had chosen their partners. Some had experienced all manner of violence and unhappiness. Some had never married. Often these were the women who seemed most idealistic of all. What, then, is the origin of this fascination?

You could say that most of society is obsessed with the idea of finding a partner, so why should elderly people be any different? A romantic ideal is constantly being presented in the media (and of course in stories), so it's easy to think, 'this was not my experience but it is possible for other people'.

For a lot of people an intimate relationship represents a major opportunity for contact. A woman I knew lost her husband to a brain tumour at fifty-six. She told me that every day of their lives together he had told her he loved her. The hardest thing about his illness was that the tumour affected his personality and for several painful months the affectionate, demonstrative man she knew disappeared. She told me of her gratitude when medication returned him to his 'old self' for a few short weeks before he died and once again he called her by her pet names and their easy intimacy returned.

The human need for contact means that the union does not necessarily have to be a happy one. People will talk about having ups and downs in their marriages and these can be quite major. I have come across elderly couples in residential homes where there has been violence between them and this poses a number of difficult problems for the staff.

Some people make contact through conflict. The image of the elderly couple who have spent a lifetime together walking hand in hand into the last stage of life is not necessarily the case for everyone. But there are definitely those who have weathered storms together and have maintained a relationship for their whole lives. What an amazing bond that must be.

Commonly, stories which focus on the securing of a partner or a love match end at the marriage. On the one hand, this can convey the illusion that all the striving takes place before the marriage or commitment to the relationship, and bliss and serenity automatically follow. Obviously, this is not the case in reality but our attachment to the type of myth that encapsulates this idea is very strong. It is often referred to in popular parlance as a 'fairy tale ending'.

Even those with the happiest of marriages will tell you of the difficulties of sustaining intimacy over time and with the changes brought by fluctuating fortunes, the arrival of children and getting older. The idea that there is one partner for life is a very attractive one even when the reality belies this. The stories look at the quest to find that partner. They do not address the challenge of keeping him or her.

Because a lot of the stories present obstacles that need to be overcome in order to win the beloved, they can represent a heroic quality that most of us can identify with which is distinct from the heroes of myth who found a kingdom or fight a battle. The presence of challenges or obstacles to be overcome also helps to make the successful union at the end very satisfying.

Of course, the attraction of these stories is not just about the very human desire for an intimate partner. Jung believed that the motif of the lovers was about the woman searching for her inner male and the man his inner female. He talked about masculine and feminine as archetypes present in us all. The masculine represents the active and dynamic within ourselves and the feminine the receptive and passive.

Part of the striving towards wholeness is a need to develop the other side of ourselves and this is not necessarily gender-based. In other words, just because I am a woman does not mean that I am comfortable being receptive and I may need to develop the more dynamic side of my personality. There are a lot of very 'feminine' men who need to contact their inner drive and women who are out of touch with their more 'passive' selves.

What can often happen is that we are attracted to a person who embodies the qualities latent within ourselves but which we are not acknowledging and we come together as two halves of a whole. This can be fine while both parties are happy to be one half of a whole. Conflicts can arise when one or both become dissatisfied with this and seek wholeness within themselves.

One of the ways to examine a story is similar to the way we can examine a dream. This would be to think of the story as the story of one person and each character represents one aspect of that person. Then we can explore how each character interacts as part of that whole person. A major attraction of a lot of these stories lies in the image of wholeness they represent.

We live at a time when gender roles are much less defined. Whenever there is a shifting in roles there is an increase in anxiety. Studies done ten years ago into the mental health of different groups of women found that the healthiest group were Hassidic women in a Jewish community in North London. This was a surprise to the researchers, who saw the women as having great restrictions put on them and not a lot of personal freedom. However, a combination of very clear roles and responsibilities and a supportive community meant that this group scored the highest in terms of mental health.

In acknowledging the presence of anxiety where gender roles are being re-evaluated and communities are breaking down, I am not advocating a return to more rigid, stereotypical roles. But an awareness of this can go some way to explaining the attraction of stories that present courtship and commitment in a relatively straightforward way.

The elderly people we work with may have had a marriage which lasted for forty or fifty years or more. This is an amazing achievement. It also means that separation will have a profound effect on both partners. Sometimes a couple go into residential care together and a lot of homes make provision for that couple to be together. I have heard, however, of one residential home where a couple were being shown to their room and as the husband went to enter the room with his wife of over fifty years he was chastised for being a 'dirty old man' and told that, 'the men's rooms are over the other side of the building'.

Often sex is a taboo subject. Old people are not supposed to be sexual and if they exhibit sexual behaviour or feelings they are labelled inappropriate. Ignorance about the nature of human sexuality leads to a lot of confused thinking. There are many myths. One is that sex is only for the young, fit and healthy. This is the myth perpetuated in the media. There is also a myth that older women lose interest in sex much quicker than men of the same age. What the research seems to point to is that our enthusiasm for sex as we get older reflects the amount of enthusiasm we've had throughout our lives.

There is also the myth that sexuality is purely the physical act of sex and this is limiting to us all. This is a popular misconception and one that can be particularly damaging to the older person.

I once attended a talk at a conference on dementia where the speaker talked for forty-five minutes about sexual behaviour in the elderly confused without once giving a definition of what she meant by 'sexual behaviour'. I think it is an indication of the fear and denial of sexual behaviour and feelings in older people that this woman presented data from the research she had done without once being specific about the focus of the research, that is, what was the definition of sexual behaviour she had used in order to carry out the research.

According to Freud, the Oedipus complex means a child is unwilling to tolerate any suggestion that the parent is sexual because it arouses sexual feelings towards the parent which the child is suppressing. Freud saw society's prudery around elderly sexuality as to do with our denial of these uncomfortable feelings of attraction towards the parent (and, by extension, people of our parents' age or generation).

Sexual behaviour includes preening and enjoying one's appearance, flirting, hugging, kissing, stroking, self-pleasuring and intercourse. Context is, as always, important. What may be considered sexual behaviour, for example a woman lifting up her skirts or a man fumbling with the fly on his trousers, may be about something different such as an urgent need to go to the loo.

A behaviour I consider sexual is not necessarily perceived in that way by someone else, which is even more reason to be very specific in the language we use to describe behaviour and not just sexual behaviour.

I co-ran a group with another woman several years ago. The group was for people with physical disabilities and learning difficulties. There was one woman in the group whose behaviour my co-worker labelled as sexual and thus avoided contact with her. This behaviour involved the woman arriving for the session and on first contact standing really close to sniff our hair. This was a woman who did not have speech and whose sight was very poor but whose sense of smell and touch was very acute. I never felt threatened by this;

in fact I quite liked the close contact. I thought it was one of the major ways that this woman recognised us and made sense of where she was. The function of the behaviour was not primarily sexual.

One of the wonderful things that stories provide is an opportunity for flirtation and all the excitement and fun that involves.

I remember a session we did using the story of 'The Blue Flower of Beechy Hill'. The group was a very established one of elderly residents in a hospital. Doris, who was in a wheelchair and almost bent double, was very clear about the role she wanted to play: 'I want to play the gypsy girl. She's sexy, that one'.

It was wonderful to see how accessible the young girl was in each of these old women and the young man in each of these old men. I also like to think that in every young girl there is the seed of the old woman waiting to emerge – that we carry within us the potential to embody each stage in our development.

In one of the places where I and another drama therapist worked for years we had a tradition of running special event sessions at Christmas and Easter. This had begun when we were asked if a few extra people could come to the session, people who normally didn't involve themselves but who might be interested in a special event. We agreed and ended up with about thirty people.

We followed a similar format to what we had been doing with our regular, smaller groups but made it more of a performance. These events were very like a pantomime but similar to the story sessions in that they weren't rehearsed.

As there were so many more people we freely called on the staff who came along to watch to help. This was great for the residents, who loved to see the staff playing roles and having fun. Of course, many of the roles were played by the residents themselves, sometimes people who had come along for the first time.

From then on, whenever there was a special occasion, such as Valentine's day, we ran a session and invited lots of people from all over the hospital to come. Sometimes we had over sixty people.

As my own wedding approached in 1992 we often wished there was a way to involve the residents. All of my elderly groups took a lot of interest in my wedding, noticeably more than other client groups who were pleased for me but didn't ask for details the way my elderly clients did.

I can't remember when we hit on the idea that if we couldn't invite residents to the wedding we could take the wedding to them. We had such a basis in role play which extended to most of the residents of the hospital and a lot of the staff, so it seemed a natural progression to role play a wedding.

We decided to 'stage' the wedding that would take place after I returned from honeymoon and where I would 'marry' Alfred, who was a regular member of the group and a popular figure throughout the hospital. From then on it was really easy to plan, as much of the wedding ritual is familiar to most people.

Sheila, the wondrous ward clerk/activities organiser, sent out handmade wedding invitations. She bought a magnum of champagne and liaised with the kitchen staff, who baked and decorated an enormous wedding cake. Residents and staff from all over the building were invited, plus relatives, friends, well wishers, volunteers and, of course, Alfred's real wife who visited every day.

The lady who worked in accounts lent an antique lace night-dress which had belonged to her grandmother for me to wear as a wedding dress. Our master of ceremonies or 'officiate' was a man who was a regular volunteer and whom everybody knew.

The residents from the secure ward for people with dementia all came wearing their Sunday best and with perfect make-up and hair. What was also interesting was that everyone behaved in a way that was perfectly appropriate for a wedding. It was almost as if the ritual was so familiar that it transcended things such as memory loss and verbal incomprehension.

We wanted there to be no confusion so we planned that the wedding take place as the climax of a story session and we had no problem finding a story that culminated in a wedding – the story of Cinderella. This was so we could have the usual convention of reminding people if there was any obvious confusion that 'it was all in the story' – that I wasn't actually marrying Alfred.

On the day, the ritual was so powerful and shared by so many people that the wedding felt real. We weren't pretending to have a wedding, we were having a wedding. Even though I was a woman in her early thirties and Alfred was in a wheelchair and forty years older there was a lack of incongruity. Even now when I look at the photos they do not strike me as odd. All the guests responded as if it were a real wedding. People were coming up to me to kiss the bride or touch the bride's gown for luck. It was a wonderful occasion for sharing and community and celebration, and something that we talked about for ages afterwards.

At Alfred's funeral several years later, members of his family who I had never met came up to speak to me. They had seen and really enjoyed the video of the wedding. His sister talked to me and held my hand. I felt like part of the family.

Of the stories I am including here, four are what I call 'loving the unlovely' stories. They are from a genre which includes 'Beauty and the Beast'. I think they are important stories to use with an elderly group or any group of people who are undervalued, unappreciated or reviled. The theme of these stories is 'look within'. Do not make assumptions on the basis of appearance as appearance can often be misleading. The stories recognise and place a high value on the 'unlovely' characters whose true nature becomes apparent through the love of another person. This is true of us all – that we blossom in an atmosphere of positive regard and acceptance.

All of the stories involve some kind of struggle or search which culminates in the finding of the 'beloved'. An opportunity to assist in a struggle, even a symbolic or metaphorical one, and have the experience of winning through at the end can be very satisfying for members of a group.

Savitri and Satyavan

There was once a princess much beloved by her parents.

When the time came for her to marry they were keen for her to make a love match so they sent portrait artists out around the kingdom to bring back likenesses of eligible men. The portraits came back of princes and rulers who were all very handsome and rich but Savitri looked at them and told her parents, 'he is not here, the one I am to marry'.

So Savitri herself set out to search throughout the cities of the world for a husband. But eventually she returned to her parents and told them, 'he is not there, the one I am to marry'. So she then organised to search throughout the forests of the world and had almost exhausted her search when one day she came upon a humble woodcutter called Satyavan. She knew immediately that he was the man for her. She told her parents, 'I have found the man I wish to marry'.

Her parents remonstrated with her, telling her that her life would be very hard as the wife of a woodcutter and she would have none of the luxuries she took for granted in the palace but Savitri's mind was made up.

Before the wedding a soothsayer was consulted to foretell the fortunes of the marriage and he had very grave news to tell: 'The man you are marrying is a good man but his stars are crossed. He has only one year and one day left to live'.

Everyone expected Savitri to cancel the wedding but she said, 'if that is all the time we have let us be married as soon as possible'. They were married and Savitri went to live as the wife of a woodcutter in the forest.

Time passed and the couple were very happy. Savitri had not forgotten the words of the soothsayer and a year and a day after they were married she insisted on accompanying Satyavan into the forest to cut wood. Satyavan tried to put her off saying, 'it will be very hot for you in the middle of the day', but she was determined so they set off together. All in the forest was still as Satyavan worked at chopping wood until after a few hours he began to complain of a terrible pain in his head.

Savitri persuaded him to lie in the cool of the banyan tree, which he did. She rested his head in her lap. Moments later Satyavan died. Savitri waited and within a short time she heard the jingle of spurs and Yama, the lord of the underworld, rode into view on his water buffalo. He took Satyavan's soul and rode off.

Savitri appealed to the banyan tree: 'keep my husband's body cool until I return with his soul', and with that she set off in pursuit of Lord Yama.

After many miles Yama turned to her and demanded to know why she was following him. 'You are taking my husband's soul, why don't you take me as well?' she asked him. Yama told her to return home and to stop bothering him.

After many more miles and admiring her determination, Yama offered her a wish. 'You can have anything you wish apart from your husband's soul,' he said. Savitri wished there was less poverty in her country and Yama agreed to her wish. Still she followed him.

After many more miles Yama turned again. 'I shall grant you one more wish then you must really go home. Remember, anything but your husband's soul.' Savitri wished to see her parents again. The wish was easily granted and the Lord rode on.

Finally, Yama began to get exasperated. He couldn't seem to shake this woman off. He decided to grant her one more wish with the usual proviso. 'I wish to be the mother of many sons,' said Savitri. 'Granted,' said Yama impatiently. 'But how can I be the mother of many sons when you have my husband's soul?' cried Savitri.

'I am exhausted with all this,' said Yama, 'here, take your husband's soul. You can have it on one condition: your own life span will be halved'.

'Agreed,' said Savitri delightedly.

'Don't you want to know how long you've got?' asked Yama, but Savitri wasn't listening. She was already making her way back to the banyan tree where she reunited Satyavan's soul with his body. Savitri thanked the banyan tree for looking after her husband's body. Satyavan opened his eyes. 'My headache has gone,' he said, 'let's go home.' Savitri agreed and the two made their way back to their home together.

Themes in the story

I find this a profoundly moving story. I particularly like the emphasis on the importance of living for the day, which features in the soothsayer's prediction that the couple have only a year and a day together and is then reiterated in the price for the release of Satyavan's soul being a halving of Savitri's life span.

Because it deals with the death of a spouse in a very direct way I would usually only use this story in a group where a lot of trust has been established.

I haven't used this story with any groups of people with dementia, simply because it is quite long and involved. However, it is a very interesting story to think about in terms of someone with a dementing illness because of the image of Satyavan, whose body is safe in the cool of the banyan tree while his soul is being carried off by the lord of death.

Dementia has been described as a living death because the person's appearance may not change significantly but their personality may be altered beyond recognition. They can be physically fit but increasingly mentally disabled. The effect of this on people who have known and loved the person is profound. It can be as if the person they knew and were familiar with has died. Certainly the type of relationship they once had may effectively be over: if a spouse, the life-long partner; if a daughter or son, the parent.

However, because the person's personality is very much changed this does not mean that they have ceased to be a person. We are so much more than just our mental faculties. This may be easier to appreciate if you have no prior history with the person.

My job as a therapist meant that I would meet people when they were already dementing so I would have no knowledge of the way they were before. To me they were simply Barbara or Dolly or Marie, each with their own distinct personality.

Michael Ignatieff's wonderful book, *Scar Tissue*[1] is a fictionalised account of his mother's dementing illness which she developed at a relatively young age. He saw her radically changed personality as a loss of self.

I can see how this could be your experience. It has not been mine. I have never met anyone without a self. I would not know what that looked like. And if we say this person has no sense of self with whom are we interacting and where has their sense of self gone? How is this going to affect the way we treat them?

The story offers wonderful suggestions. In order for Savitri to bring those parts of her husband together she had to travel a long way and be very persistent and very patient. (The image of the wife working to bring together parts of the husband that have been severed occurs in Egyptian mythology in the story of Isis and Osiris. In that story, the dead body of Osiris was dismembered and the parts scattered all over Egypt. Isis, in the form of a swallow, flew throughout the land searching for, and then piecing back together, her husband's broken body.)

Often in working with people with dementia who are very withdrawn or confused, we have to be prepared to be patient and creative in the ways we use to attempt to make contact. The persistence comes when we continue to make this effort, even when the response seems to be very small or

---

1   Michael Ignatieff (1993) *Scar Tissue*. London: Vintage.

non-existent. We can recognise that the person is choosing or is simply not in a place to make contact with us at that time, but that this may change. We need to be prepared to keep the doors of communication open for the person, ready for the moment when they choose to step through.

This story very graphically demonstrates the other side of loving, which is the possibility of losing the one we love. Often people guard against this loss by refusing to love or become emotionally involved. The story shows the courage needed to choose a partner you love even when you know you have little time. Savitri could have chosen another suitor but she preferred to make the most of the time she had with the one she really wanted. In this she refused to compromise.

In the short term her lifestyle was changed out of all recognition and the story presents a view of love that transcends class and social status. It is her lifestyle that must change. The story is clear that Satyavan does not give up being a woodcutter and go and live in the palace. Savitri must endure hardship and adapt herself in order to be with the one she loves.

There are similarities with 'The blue flower of Beechy Hill' in that the stories involve a search for the beloved and present an ideal image of what the spouse should be. This story rejects status, looks and money in favour of a good man.

There is also Savitri's instinctive recognition of the suitable spouse and her parents' support of this despite Satyavan's obvious shortcomings in terms of wealth and prestige. Is it coincidence that Savitri, who has parents described as very loving and supportive of her search and choice, is very clear and confident in who she wants for a mate?

Using the story in a session

When I did this story with a youthful elderly group it stimulated a great deal of discussion. People really agreed with the importance of having a loving husband or wife. One woman told me, 'It's the most important thing. As long as you've got a good husband you don't need anything else'.

Jack, who had never married, talked for the first time of a woman he had loved in his youth. The story seemed to bring up some feelings of regret for him that he had not let himself experience the sort of commitment described in the story.

One woman talked of her first husband, who had died soon after they had married. She had subsequently remarried several times but the image of her first husband remained as an ideal.

One group loved the part about Savitri winning back her husband's soul but were outraged at the price she had to pay – half of her own life. They thought that Savitri had paid enough in her pursuit of Yama without having to forfeit half her own life for the return of her husband. Being so familiar with a number of underworld myths from other cultures I was not surprised there was a price. There is always a huge price if someone is to be filched from the mouth of death.

I wonder if our different attitudes towards this point had to do with us being at very different points on the life line. The thought of forfeiting half your life span for the one you love may not seem too daunting when you are young and think you have all the time in the world. Maybe you have a very different concept of time when you're well into the last third of the average life span. Maybe I will feel very differently about this aspect of the story when I am in my sixties and seventies.

Savitri knows instantly that Satyavan is the one for her. I would often ask people, 'do you believe in love at first sight?'. I was amazed at how many people did.

In an enactment of this story with a group of people who had had strokes, a woman played the banyan tree which shelters the body of Satyavan, played by another resident, a man whose sight was impaired. We arranged her wheelchair so that Michael could lean across her and she put her arms around him. He let himself rest on her until the part where his body and soul are reunited. There were jokes at first at how quiet he was as Michael was usually extremely ebullient and outgoing, particularly enjoying heroic parts or ones involving royalty such as kings or emperors. I really loved how much integrity he had when playing the part. He didn't joke around but had a real dignity which made the enactment very moving and powerful.

Coming from India the story provided a wonderful opportunity for me to bring in a couple of saris I had bought very cheaply in a shop in East London. They were of the brightest, most iridescent colours and my youthful elderly group had great fun trying them on and working out how to wear them.

For my frailer group we encouraged people to try the saris around them like shawls. We also made a little palanquin out of them and wafted them over people's heads. We were really trying to give people the experience of feeling like empresses or maharajahs.

In one group, nobody offered to take the part of Yama, the Lord of Death, so I asked my assistant, a young male nurse, if he would take the role. He took to the part with gusto and when he arrived on his 'water buffalo' he announced himself in a loud voice: 'I am Yama, Lord of Death', to which one old lady who had a very dry sense of humour replied, 'well, don't think I'm afraid of you, dear, I'm too old'.

Gawain and Lady Ragnell

One day while King Arthur was out hunting alone he came across a fierce knight called Sir Gromer, who demanded the return of some lands of his or revenge for his loss. He agreed to spare Arthur if he could give him the answer to a question: 'what is it that women most desire above all else?'. He gave Arthur a year in which to find the answer and made arrangements to meet him in exactly the same spot in a year's time or Arthur would forfeit his life.

Arthur returned to the court very shaken by the experience and told his knights what had transpired.

They were outraged at Sir Gromer's impudence and set out immediately to all corners of the kingdom to find the answer to the question.

The knights travelled far and wide in every direction, but as the year passed away none came back with answers that had the ring of truth.

As the day drew near when Arthur was to meet Sir Gromer, he was again alone in the forest when he came upon a most loathsome lady.

She introduced herself as Lady Ragnell and said she was the half sister of Sir Gromer. She said that she knew Arthur did not have the answer to Sir Gromer's question but that she did, and she would tell him on the condition that Sir Gawain became her husband.

Now Gawain was Arthur's nephew and a great favourite at the court. Arthur could not imagine marrying his young, handsome knight to such a grotesque-looking old woman and said so. 'You misunderstand me,' said Lady Ragnell, 'I did not suggest forcing Sir Gawain into the match. He must choose of his own free will. Those are my terms. I shall meet you here tomorrow to hear your decision.'

With that she disappeared into the forest leaving Arthur feeling very dismayed.

When he returned to the court he was reluctant to tell Gawain Lady Ragnell's terms but eventually he did and he was amazed at the young man's response. 'I would be delighted to marry her if it may save your life!'

The next day they rode out together to meet Lady Ragnell. Gawain pledged to marry her very gallantly and the lady looked well pleased at the match. They then received the answer to the all-important question.

Armed with this information Arthur journeyed to met Sir Gromer in the agreed spot with a lighter heart. 'Well,' said Sir Gromer, 'have you the answer to my question?' Arthur gave a few wrong answers first until Sir Gromer began to lift up his great sword to cleave the king in two. 'Stop,' said Arthur. 'Now I remember, what a woman desires most of all is sovereignty over her own life and the freedom to exercise her own will.'

Sir Gromer saw at once that this was the correct answer and in a fury he swung up his sword and rode off into the forest.

Back at court the wedding of the loathsome lady and her sweet knight took place and in due course the couple retired to their bedchamber.

There Lady Ragnell demanded a kiss which Gawain freely gave her. And what a transformation occurred! As Gawain stepped back he saw before him a fair and lovely woman.

'What manner of sorcery is this?' he exclaimed.

'Do not be afraid husband,' Lady Ragnell replied. 'My half brother Sir Gromer had me turned into a loathsome lady that could only be transformed if the greatest knight in England willingly married me. This you have done so you see me in my natural form. However, you now have a choice. What would you have me, loathsome by day and lovely by night or lovely by day and loathsome by night? Think carefully before you choose.'

Gawain thought carefully for a moment then replied, 'Dearest, this is not a choice for me to make, it is for you to choose. I shall abide by whatever decision you make'.

> With that she kissed him delightedly and said, 'there is the last of the spell broken, for Sir Gromer said that if when married to the greatest knight in England he gave me sovereignty over my own life I would be free of all enchantment'.
>
> And with that the couple embraced and lived happily ever after.

Themes in the story

The crone in fairy stories is very often a malevolent force opposed to the heroes and heroines, who are often very youthful. It is the image of the spiteful old person who is jealous of youth. I tend to avoid stories that present the crone in this way.

She is also often a peripheral, although catalytic, figure (as is the mysterious wise old man).

One of the things I like about this story is that Lady Ragnell is a major and intriguing character.

In ancient cultures the crone was one aspect of the triple-faced goddess, the other two aspects being the young girl and the mother. She was associated with old age and death and the inevitable dissolution and reorganisation which must occur before regeneration can take place.

The crone also represented the third, post-menopausal stage in women's lives and was venerated as such, as it was believed that women became very wise when they no longer shed the lunar or wise blood but kept it within.

The influence of Christianity devalued the crone and elevated the mother in the figure of the Virgin Mary (although one could argue that the symbol of the Virgin Mary successfully combines the mother with the image of the young girl/virgin). By the Middle Ages, and the time of this story, we can see how the crone is fully devalued, and the witch hunts in Europe were a shocking example of this – some research says that 93 per cent of those indicted and found guilty were women and many of these were old women living on their own.

In the 1990s we live in a culture obsessed with the image of the young girl – only one side of the goddess triptych remains as an object of veneration.

In the story of Gawain and Lady Ragnell the crone is portrayed as loathsome and repulsive. She is also the possessor of great power. She is the only one in the kingdom who can supply Arthur with the answer to the question he needs and thus save his life. She is capable of transforming herself and there are many stories where association or confrontation with a crone leads to an internal transformation in the hero or heroine. Baba Yaga in a Russia folk tale is a frightening and exciting figure. She has iron teeth and flies through the air in a cauldron. Her house is supported on giant chicken legs like stilts and has a fence made out of human bones lit by lights within human skulls. Vassilissa is tricked by her uncaring step mother and step sisters and has to go into the forest to fetch fire from the house of Baba Yaga. Not only does she survive the ordeal but through her resourcefulness and courage she triumphs. Dakinis or sky dancers are hags in Tibetan mythology who danced in graveyards and rode through the sky with streaming black hair and blood red skin. The Bodhisatva Padmasambhava engaged their anarchic energy and they became guardians of the Dharma or Buddhist teaching.

Like so many of the 'loving the unlovely' stories, the hero or heroine has to marry willingly and with good grace. In this way the story signals a need for that heroic part of ourselves to be very open and receptive to other possibilities.

Using the story in a session

Very often the majority of my elderly groups comprised women and this story provoked a lot of discussion and laughter. The part of Lady Ragnell was very popular. One woman said, 'I want to play the old hag who gets the young man – I've always fancied a toy boy'.

With most groups I would pose the question, 'what do women want?'. Then it would be in people's minds when in the enactment the knights are despatched throughout the kingdom to find the answer. This is a way of involving people who are happy to watch and contribute verbally but do not want to take a role.

The responses to this question varied. Some people said 'money', others 'a good man'. One man said ruefully, 'to be the boss'. However, when the answer was provided in the story most people seemed to think it was a good one.

I would also ask the other question in the story, 'would you want the person lovely by day and loathsome by night or loathsome by day and lovely by night?'. This inspired a number of amusing replies.

The Blue Flower of Beechy Hill

On Beechy Hill, it was said, there grew a blue flower that conferred great health and happiness on whosoever discovered it.

One day a shepherd called Eric was grazing his sheep on the hill when he came upon a large blue flower. Reaching down he plucked it and was amazed to find standing beside him an old man with a long beard clutching a shepherd's staff.

'Eric, I know you to be a fine man, well deserving of the good fortune coming your way. You will be an honest leader for the people around these parts. Here, take these two bags of gold that will never be empty and go to the top of the hill to find your castle. The one thing I cannot give you is a wife. You must choose your life's companion yourself but the blue flower will help you to choose wisely.' With that the old man disappeared.

Eric tucked the flower into his lapel and made his way up the hill where sure enough stood a castle full of servants who welcomed him as their lord. Eric tucked his gold away safely in his chamber, helped himself to fine clothes from his closet and, going to the stables, picked out a strong, black horse for a journey. He told the servants he would not be back for some time and then rode off in search of a bride.

The first thing he came upon was a country fair. He got himself a room and washed and changed into smart clothes. In the evening he went to the dance that was full of pretty girls. He danced all night with a flame haired beauty and during a merry reel he asked her, 'How would you like to live in a fine castle?'. The girl replied immediately, 'I would love to, then I could sit and eat cake and do nothing all day'. Eric glanced at the blue flower in his lapel and heard it say, 'no, no, no'. With that he decided to move on.

In the course of his travels he stopped one night at a big house. 'I'm a traveller, can you give me shelter?' The master of the house made him welcome and he dined that night with the family and the master's three lovely daughters. He ended up staying for a few days and spent a lot of time with the eldest.

She was as accomplished as she was beautiful. She played the harpsichord and spoke French. One day, as they were sitting companionably together, Eric asked her if cooking was among her accomplishments. 'Cooking! That is lowly servant's work. I would not soil my pretty hands with such a thing.' With that Eric turned to the flower in his lapel to hear it saying, 'no, no, no'. Eric took his leave of the family and rode on.

One afternoon Eric was caught in a thunderstorm. In the distance he saw a humble cottage with a young woman sitting in the window. He made for the cottage and was received graciously by the girl, whose name was Gudula. She explained that she lived there and cared for her father. She offered Eric hospitality and a warm place beside the fire for the night. Soon her father came home and the three sat down for a meal.

Eric ended up staying a week and found himself becoming more and more enamoured of Gudula and she of him. She had a kindness and gentleness which more than made up for her plain appearance.

At the end of the week he asked her father for her hand in marriage. As he did so he heard the flower on his lapel sing out, 'yes, yes, yes'.

The two were married and Eric took her back to his castle where they lived happily ever after.

Themes in the story

A major theme in this English story is the recognition and reward for someone's worth.

There are similarities with the story of Aaron in 'The Bird of Happiness' in that Eric is elevated from very humble origins to a position of great power and responsibility. The blue flower is similar to the glowing stone in the Jewish story in that it guides him to make the wise decisions that will influence his future and he allows himself to be guided.

I found that people found the idea of having no more money worries very attractive. Most of the people I worked with were working people who had often had to struggle to make ends meet. A lot of them had grown up in the 1930s at the time of the Depression and I think people inherited a horror of that situation ever happening again. Certainly stories that involved big sacks of gold seemed to go down very well!

It's very much a story that offers an image of courtship that people can relate to. A lot of people went to dances, went for walks, spent time getting to know one another before committing to each other. People agreed it was important to choose the right person. Nowadays more and more people, particularly men, wait until they have established themselves in a job, career and lifestyle before they commit themselves to finding a long-term partner. This story gives us a model of that particular approach by having Eric's material needs magically taken care of which leaves him with the task of finding someone with which to share his good fortune.

The story raises the question of what makes a good wife. Eric is the recipient of good fortune but he has also inherited responsibilities as new lord of the castle and the surrounding areas. His wife, then, must be someone who can share those responsibilities.

Using the story in a session

One group particularly liked Gudula being very unassuming looking. One woman said, 'I didn't think my husband was at all good looking when I first married him but he was very kind. And you know, as he got older he became really handsome. I don't know if that was just me or what'.

Some people were very pragmatic. They thought romantic love was relatively unimportant. They really favoured qualities of stability and reliability.

Some of the women were very critical of the girl who was accomplished but couldn't cook (and was also unwilling to learn). One said, 'what use is playing the harpsichord if there's no food on the table?'.

In one group Eric was played by a man in a wheelchair. For the journey, the co-therapist pushed 'Eric' round the room in his chair and returned to the semi-circle for different scenes. The story begins on Beechy Hill and then Eric journeys up the hill to find his castle. So George was wheeled out of the circle as he left the hill and back in again when he came upon the castle, and so on.

We had a tradition of hand dancing in the group which is a way of dancing with people while they are sitting down. When it came to the dance in the story we took the opportunity to go round and invite everyone to the country dance.

When 'Eric' meets and dances with the gypsy girl – played by Doris, also in a wheelchair – we manoeuvred their chairs so they were opposite each other and side by side. This way they could hand dance with each other and flirt a little. At the end of the dance 'Eric' gallantly took the gypsy girl's hand and kissed it.

The Black Bull of Norway

There was once an old woman who had three daughters. She worked night and day to keep them fed and clothed and they always looked really well turned out and had lovely manners and were a credit to her.

Eventually they grew restless and wanted to be out in the world so the eldest said, 'I'm going down to the valley'.

She went and stayed in the cottage of a wise woman and her only daughter, who said to her, 'stay here tonight and in the morning look out of the back door and see what comes'.

The girl did as she was bid and in the morning looked out of the back door and what should she see coming but a glass coach drawn by six horses. The wise woman asked her what she could see and she replied, 'a glass coach coming drawn by six fine horses'. 'That's coming for you,' said the wise woman and the girl tripped out to the coach in high excitement. The coachman opened the door for her and helped her in.

Soon the second sister began getting restless and one morning she announced, 'I'm going down to the valley to see what I can see'. Off she went to the cottage of the wise woman and her only daughter, who bade her stay the night and in the morning look out of the back door and say what she saw. This the girl did and what should she see coming but a silver carriage drawn by four greys. The wise woman asked her what she saw and she replied, 'a silver carriage drawn by four fine greys'.

'That's coming for you,' said the wise woman and the girl ran out to meet the coach and was helped inside by the coachman.

Finally the third and youngest daughter, whose name was Flora, decided to go down to the valley to see what she could see.

Instructed by the wise woman she stayed the night and in the morning looked out of the back door. But what should she see lumbering down the valley but an enormous black bull. The wise woman asked her what she saw and Flora replied, 'a black bull is coming and it's big'. 'He's coming for you,' replied the wise woman. 'For me!' said Flora with dismay. The bull was an ugly beast with broad shoulders and a hairy neck and the wise woman helped Flora on his back and away he went.

Soon Flora's fear gave way to curiosity. She began to enjoy the journey and looked around her at the countryside, which was becoming rocky and mountainous. 'I'm hungry,' she said. The beast replied, 'look in my right ear'. Flora did and there was food. 'I'm thirsty,' she said. 'Look in my left ear,' said the bull. She did and there was drink. Flora ate and drank and was wonderfully refreshed.

Soon they came in sight of a wondrous castle made of stone. 'We'll stay there tonight,' said the bull, 'this is the castle of my eldest brother.' 'Who are you then?' asked Flora. But the bull didn't answer as he thundered on up to the castle gates.

That night Flora slept in a four poster bed while the bull was put in a pasture. In the morning she was shown in to breakfast with the master of the castle, who was holding a shiny red apple. 'You are welcome here,' he said, 'take this apple but only break it open when you have dire need of it.'

After breakfast, Flora was lifted back up on to the bull's back and away they went.

They travelled all day and as evening fell they came within sight of a castle covered with pennants and flags of many colours. 'We'll stay here tonight,' said the bull, 'it's the castle of my elder brother'. 'So, who are you?' asked Flora, but the bull said nothing.

After a night spent in comfort, Flora was shown to the breakfast room of the lord of the castle who said to her, 'you are welcome here. Take this pear but only open it in dire need'. Flora thanked him and she and the bull set off for another day of travelling.

The landscape was becoming increasingly barren and desolate looking as they sped on.

At the evening of the third day they came within sight of a castle made entirely of painted wood.

'We'll stop here,' said the bull, 'this is the castle of my younger brother.' Again Flora asked him, 'well, who are you?'. But the bull did not reply.

The next day Flora shared breakfast with the lord of the castle, who showed her a luscious plum. 'You are welcome here, Flora,' he said, 'and this is for you. Only open it, however, when you are in dire need.' Flora thanked the man and set off on the bull's back once more.

On they went until they came to a dark and fearsome valley, strewn with boulders with a small stream running through it. 'Wait here,' said the bull, 'I must go and fight the devil. Stay on this rock and move not a muscle. If everything around you turns blue it means I'll have beaten him. If all turns red, it'll mean that he has beaten me. Remember, whatever happens, do not move, otherwise I won't be able to find you.'

Flora did as she was bade. She sat as still as a mouse for what seemed like hours until all of a sudden she noticed the water in the stream had turned a bright blue. Unable to contain her excitement she crossed one foot over the other.

When the bull returned he couldn't find her, though he searched for days.

In vain Flora searched for him but eventually she gave up and after many days she returned to the house of the wise woman and her daughter. 'Oh, so you've come back,' said the wise woman. 'A young knight is staying here who says whoever can wash his shirt free of bloodstains can be his wife.' 'Can you or your daughter not clean the shirt?' said Flora. 'No, we cannot and you must try. Here is the shirt.'

The woman insisted Flora wash the shirt and when she did the shirt washed clean and new without a trace of bloodstain.

Then Flora was so tired after her journey that she fell fast asleep on her bed and missed the return of the knight.

The wise woman took the shirt and told the knight that it was her daughter who had washed it clean. 'Well then,' said the knight, 'it is she I must marry', and the wise woman began to make preparations for the wedding.

When Flora awoke she was appalled to find out what had happened and when she saw the handsome knight with his broad shoulders and curly black hair she said to herself, 'I know you', but the wedding to the wise woman's daughter was set for that day and she despaired of being able to do anything to stop it.

In her room she remembered the apple. She broke it open and inside were precious gems. She went to the wise woman's daughter and said, 'I'll give you these jewels if you postpone the wedding until tomorrow and let me go into the knight's room tonight. The greedy girl agreed but the exchange had been witnessed by the wise woman, who made sure the knight had a flagon of ale before retiring which was full of sleeping potion.

That night, Flora slipped into the knight's room and, crouching down beside him, she reminded him of the journey they had made together and how she had searched for him and that she loved him. But the knight slept on and heard nothing.

The next day in desperation Flora broke open the pear and found inside it jewels even more precious than before. She approached the wise woman's daughter, who agreed to postpone the wedding for one more day and let her go into the knight's room. But again the wise woman drugged the knight's drink and again he was insensible to Flora's declarations.

Again Flora sank into despair but she remembered the plum and, breaking it open, she found jewels that outshone all the others.

Again the wise woman's daughter agreed to her request and Flora knew it was her last chance. However, the knight had grown suspicious of the wise woman's night-time drink and had managed to avoid drinking it. When Flora slipped into his room he was fully conscious to hear the words she whispered to him. Flora was delighted when the knight sat up in bed and embraced her. She told him all that had befallen her and he told her all that had befallen him.

The next day they were married and lived happily ever after.

Themes in the story

This version is précised from a much longer version. In the original, after Flora inadvertently moves and the bull cannot find her after he successfully fights the devil, she undergoes seven years of hardship before she returns to the wise woman's house and meets the knight.

The original story also differs in that it has the knight ordering that the wise woman and her daughter are trussed up and burned to death! I usually ask groups what they think we should do with the wise woman and her daughter. They rarely advocate anything as violent. Most people tend to think if you've got your man you can afford to be generous.

There is a theme of recognition and lack of recognition in the story, an image of two people missing each other. On the ride through the countryside Flora keeps asking the black bull, 'who are you?' She can see who his brothers are but not him. Because Flora does not obey the strict instruction that she not move (she momentarily loses concentration), when the bull returns after successfully conquering the devil (his inner demons?) he is unable to find her. Only when she has endured much does she recognise the knight as her beloved and then it is almost too late. At this point, he doesn't recognise her – he has the wool pulled over his eyes by the trickery of the wise woman and the drugged drink. In this way the story is signalling a lack of awareness, the knight has lost consciousness. This theme of not recognising the beloved is the story's way of describing a psychological concept called projection. We often fail to see who a person really is because we are too busy projecting our own fantasises on to that person. This is particularly common in romantic relationships, where the process of falling in love could be described as a massive exercise in projection by both partners. As we spend more time with a person and begin to get to know them it's less easy to project on to them. Often there is a stage that follows where people either begin to build a real relationship based on who each of them are or they move on to new partners.

The three brothers each give Flora a different fruit which contains gems that greatly assist her. The image of something commonplace containing something extremely valuable is common in stories and is a very positive image to use with groups.

Using the story in a session

The group was well established. Most people were in wheelchairs and there was a lot of contact between members of the group. People made specific requests of who they would like to sit next to and waved to each other across the circle.

For the objects I had a wooden apple which opened into two pieces that people really liked. I also brought in an old frilly shirt which I introduced by saying, 'in the story the girl has to get blood out of a shirt, any ideas on how to do that?'. This question gave loads of scope for affirming people's experience and knowledge.

When I told the story for the first time people started to pick up on the refrain of Flora's question to the bull, 'and who are you?'. By the time I got to the part where Flora realises the identity of the knight there was a lot of laughter, particularly in the description of the knight as being swarthy and thick set.

In the enactment the part of the black bull was taken by Alfred, who through a stroke could no longer speak. He was tremendously expressive with a keen sense of humour and the most wonderful blue eyes which he used to great comical effect.

Adie, a young care assistant, played the role of Flora and hung on to the handles of his wheelchair to simulate the thundering journey through the countryside.

When she lent down to take food from Alfred's ear, he pulled the most astonished expression at the food she was miming that everyone fell about laughing.

The sexual connotations of the girl riding a bull were even more obvious in the enactment when the 'girl' was actually hanging on to the back of Alfred's wheelchair. This was partly because he kept rolling his eyes every time the narrator said, 'and Flora rode the black bull through the countryside'.

Tam Lin

There was a young woman who lived in a village beside a dell that was reputed to be enchanted and full of fairies. Most people avoided going through it and told their children not to play in it but this young woman often strolled in it, admiring the wild flowers and the shafts of sunlight that came slanting through the branches of the trees and the ferns.

One day, when she was out walking, she met a young man. They struck up a conversation and enjoyed a very pleasant afternoon together and made an arrangement to meet in the same place the following day. She asked him his name and he told her, 'Tam Lin'.

After a very short time of these secret meetings the couple made their feelings known to one another, but Tam Lin hung his head and looked very sad. 'What is it, my love?' asked the young girl, fearing in her heart some obstacle to their being together.

Then Tam Lin told her his story. 'I was born in the same village as you,' he said, 'but abducted by fairies when I was a tiny baby. I belong to the fairy queen and she would never willingly let me go.' 'But is there no way to release you?' exclaimed the girl. 'There is but one way,' replied Tam Lin.

'Once a year on Hallows Eve, the fairy band go riding by the crossroads at midnight. If you were to be there and drag me off my horse and hold me for the count of twelve while the church bells chime, my enchantment would be broken. You would need to hold me no matter what, for if you let go I shall be lost to you forever.' The girl replied, 'Old Hallows Eve is tomorrow night and I shall wait for you by the crossroads and hold on to you no matter what'.

The girl did as she had been instructed by Tam Lin and at midnight was waiting by the crossroads. All at once she heard a jingling of harness and the pounding of hooves and into sight came the fairy band with the fairy queen at the head.

She almost forgot herself for a moment so splendid was the spectacle, but then she caught sight of Tam Lin riding towards the back of the entourage. As he passed by she pulled him from his horse and hung on for dear life as the bells began to chime midnight.

As soon as she realised what was happening the fairy queen whirled around on her steed and set a powerful spell on Tam Lin that turned him into a mass of writhing snakes.

The girl was horrified and had to fight her revulsion and the desire to drop what she was holding as quickly as she could. But she managed to hang on.

Furious, the fairy queen sent another powerful spell that turned Tam Lin into a lump of boiling hot iron that seared the girl's flesh and burnt her badly. But still she hung on.

Finally the clock chimed its last and the queen, realising she had lost, turned Tam Lin back into his own fair self and the fairy band disappeared into the mist.

The couple embraced one another and Tam Lin thanked the girl and took her down to the stream where he bathed her poor hands. Then they made their way back to the village where they were married and lived happily ever after.

Themes in the story

When I first started working in places for elderly people I was struck by how little physical touching there was. Sometimes there would be obvious affection from one of the staff to one of the residents and occasionally there was a friendship between residents which meant that they would never go anywhere without the other. Yet the amount of physical contact you would normally see and experience, even in our undemonstrative country, was absent.

What I also noticed was how many residents would reach out to touch my face or stroke my hand so it was obvious the desire for touch was there. I decided to find stories that gave an opportunity for touching, holding and being held and 'Tam Lin' was one of these.

The young man in the story is not free to have a relationship with the girl he loves. He is under a spell. The image of the spellbound lover is common in stories and can have many meanings. One interpretation is that the young man is bound in his relationship to his mother. The fairy queen is not his natural mother but she stole him as a child and raised him as one of her own. It is a delicate operation to prise someone out of over-attachment to a parent of the opposite sex. Jungians would describe this as having a mother complex, which can be extremely destructive. In the story, the girl has to hold on to Tam Lin despite all the manipulations and manoeuvres of the queen. Only when he has undergone many changes is he free of the enchantment.

Using the story in a session

I incorporated the theme of holding present in the story into the warm-up or limber. Often older people, particularly those who have been ill, miss the opportunity to feel their physical strength and the pleasure and confidence that it can bring. In this group most people were in wheelchairs and had had strokes which affected one, and sometimes both, sides of the body. This meant that although one side of the body was paralysed, the other side was often very strong. I have met a lot of people in wheelchairs with great upper body strength. Anything that utilises that strength in a fun and contactful way is good.

With this story I asked people to experiment with different ways of holding using hands. I rearranged people's wheelchairs so that pairs of people were within easy distance of one another. In this way I also facilitated contact between individual members of the group.

I was aware that one woman in the group did not like close physical contact so we used one of the props to give her an experience of holding on and the physical strength needed to do so. I had brought in a piece of bright green material which had quite a lot of lycra in it. This was ostensibly to remind people of the brightness of green in the countryside, as many people hadn't been out for years. But also lycra has the wonderful quality of elasticity which means you can pull on it as much as you like and it won't tear. In a circle we each held on to a portion of the fabric which stretched it across the circle and pulled as hard as we could. Some people's grip was so strong they would never let go and they looked really pleased. For those who were feeling frail or whose grip was not so strong there were helpers who could support them. There are lots of permutations on the lycra stretched across the circle which are great fun and which also really extend people's movement vocabulary. One is to bounce a ball or a bean bag on the lycra.

What I have also done is to have a person held by members of the group which can be really good fun. In one group, I was assisted by a nurse who was much loved by the residents. Two group members held her around the waist and arms while I struggled to pull her away. Obviously we are not aiming to have a full-scale wrestling match but I didn't find it easy to pull her away because they were both strong and determined and held on really tightly.

In a group of people who were dementing and on a day when the energy level seemed very low, I focused on the other opportunity this story presents, which is of holding and being held in a more tender way. In the limber, myself and my co-worker went round the group and said something like, 'in the story the girl has to hold on tight to her lover to stop him being spirited away – so she really has to hug him, can I give you a hug?'. Most people laughed and said, 'if you like' or if non-verbal lifted up their arms towards us. People were very clear in their body language if they didn't want a hug and we would never dream of forcing them. Some people really hugged us back and many seemed reluctant to let us go so we tried to give them as much time as they needed.

In the enactment of the story I had the chance to enlist the group's help to hang on to Tam Lin so that people can experience holding as well as being held, and helping as well as commonly being the one who is helped (which is many people's experience once they become old and frail).

Of course, you do not need to have a story which focuses on this theme in order to cuddle or be cuddled by your clients.

I remember an enactment of the Greek story of Atalanta, who is abandoned as a baby and left to be reared by bears. I was playing the role of Atalanta as a baby in a group of people with dementia. I was on the floor trying to give a convincing impersonation of a baby's cry when Mary, who had actually been very quiet and withdrawn throughout the session and who had been sitting with her arms crossed, bent down and urged me to sit up on the seat beside her. She was making the cooing sounds you use to communicate with a small baby and she cuddled me and she stroked my hair. I really enjoyed the contact and when I 'grew up' into the adult Atalanta Mary was a lot more involved and animated.

Another occasion with the same group was when one of our most regular and dearest clients was seriously ill. For the last two sessions before she died she joined the group and was very, very low in energy. She sat and was cuddled throughout the session by one of us while the other ran the group. Often she appeared to be sleeping but seemed to enjoy being held and made it clear that she wanted to be there. We were really sad when we learned of her death but happy that we had managed to have that contact with her before she died.

Another story I used that gave opportunities for holding was an Indian myth.

In this story, Amrita is a young woman who loves trees and the forest beside the village where she lives. She loves the trees so much that she often goes to hug them and has her favourites. One day the maharajah orders his axemen to chop down the forest in order to find wood for a new palace. Amrita is appalled and organises the villagers to go into the forest and wrap their arms around a tree to stop it being chopped down by the axemen. In frustration the axemen vow to return. The villagers celebrate their victory but it is shortlived, as soon the axemen return with the maharajah and his entourage. He demands to see the perpetrator of this crime of disobedience and defiance of the crown. Amrita steps forward. The maharajah cannot believe his eyes: 'such a little slip of a thing causing too much trouble'. He is about to issue a proclamation when a wind blows up – a terrible storm which blows the sand in from the desert. Everyone takes cover among the trees while the storm blows over. Eventually people are able to emerge from the cover of the forest, brushing the sand out of their faces and dusting down their clothes. The maharajah now has a great insight into the importance of the forest in protecting the village and its people from the elements. He rescinds his orders and leaves. Amrita and the villagers are overjoyed and celebrate for many days.

This is a really good story to use in a new group where people may feel self-conscious about playing a big role. There is plenty of opportunity for people to play villagers or trees. It has echoes of David and Goliath stories where a 'little' person is up against a huge adversary. A lot of older people can identify with being in this position.

The Frog Princess

There was once a king who had three sons and the time came for them to marry.

So he took them out to the balcony of the palace and handed each his bow and arrows and said to them, 'fire off an arrow and wherever it lands there shall be your bride'.

At once the eldest son took an arrow and, bending back his bow, let fly an arrow that landed in the garden of a wealthy banker who had a lovely daughter. Everyone cheered and the eldest son was well pleased with his bride.

The second son took his bow and arrow and his arrow landed in the garden of a prosperous merchant who had a very beautiful daughter, who was delighted to marry a prince. Again the crowd cheered as they looked a very fine couple.

The youngest son got all excited and fired off an arrow that missed the village and landed in the neighbouring swamp instead. After a few minutes, out from the swamp hopped a little frog with the arrow in her mouth. 'There's your bride,' said the king and the boy's heart fell. He looked at the fine girls of his brothers with their dainty hands and feet and shining hair and flashing eyes, and he looked at the green skin and bulging eyes of his bride and he could have wept.

However, all three brothers were married and took up residence in the palace with their new wives.

Now, soon after the wedding the king decided to test his new daughters-in-law so he called them to him and he said, 'daughters, I want to see which one of you can bake the best bread. I want the softest, whitest bread for my breakfast tomorrow'.

So the three went off and neither the banker's daughter nor the merchant's daughter had any experience of baking bread so they threw flour and dough around for a bit and came up with a couple of loaves of bread.

However, the frog princess waited until nightfall and then she hopped down to the royal kitchen and invoked the help of a band of fairies, so that the next morning the frog princess delivered the most delicious freshly baked bread to the king for his breakfast. The king sampled all three breads and pronounced the frog princess's the best.

The youngest son was delighted but his spirits fell when his father the king announced another challenge for the young brides.

'Daughters,' he said, 'I want each of you to sew me a shirt, as fine a shirt as I wore on my name day. I want it here tomorrow for me to wear to breakfast.'

Immediately the banker's daughter and the merchant's daughter set to with needle and thread and although their fingers were very nimble they had had no schooling or experience in sewing and their efforts were very lacklustre.

The frog princess, however, waited until the dead of night and then she hopped down to the royal kitchens where the band of fairies helped her to make the most wondrous, embroidered shirt, which they worked on all night.

In the morning the king carefully examined the efforts of his daughters-in-law. His eyes lit up when he unfolded the shirt of the frog princess and he announced it the best of all. The youngest son hugged his wife but his spirits fell when the king announced his final challenge. 'I am going to throw a ball and invite the finest families in the land,' he said, 'and I would like to see which of my daughters-in-law is the best dancer.' The banker's daughter and the merchant's daughter heaved a sigh of relief. Here at last was something that they had both been schooled in. The youngest son looked at his wife and he thought, 'I don't know how she baked the bread or how she made the shirt but there is no way that she is ever going to be able to dance. I will be a laughing stock'.

The evening of the ball arrived and the youngest son was miserable. The frog princess kissed him and said, 'you go along to the ball and I will follow in a little while'.

When he had left she slipped off her frog skin and emerged as a beautiful woman. Arriving at the ball she created quite a stir. The youngest son was overcome with joy. He twirled her round the dance floor and she was a wonderful dancer. The king named her as the best dancer out of the three daughters-in-law and the youngest son's happiness was complete.

Towards the end of the evening he whispered to her, 'I'm going to go back to our apartments. Meet me there in half an hour'.

He returned home, found the frog skin and threw it on the fire.

When the princess returned and found the frog skin was destroyed she was very sad. She explained to the prince, 'I was under an enchantment that was to have ended within several days. If only you had not burned the frog skin. Now this means that I will have to leave you'.

The prince pleaded with her to stay but she was adamant. She left the palace and disappeared.

The prince sent out emissaries throughout the kingdom but no one had any news of her. Finally he set out himself to search for her.

His search took him many years and across many lands until after twenty years he found himself back in his home land. He made his way to his father's palace and who should he see at the threshold but his dearly beloved princess. The two embraced each other, older and wiser. They walked back inside arm in arm and began their life together.

Themes in the story

This is a Russian story although other cultures have very similar versions. I adapted it to suit my elderly groups because it was extremely long and involved. I diverge from the original at the point that the princess leaves after the burning of the frog skin. In the Russian version the story then focuses on the trials and tribulations the prince has to undergo in order to deserve his princess. At the end of these and after many years he has attained the maturity needed in order to be with her. I wanted the story to be shorter and simpler while acknowledging the need for the young prince to mature. The trials and tribulations of the Russian version achieve this effect and in cutting them out I had to replace them with something else. In the end I decided to have a circular journey (the myth of the return journey is a common motif in stories and it makes psychological sense – it's basically saying that what we search for is often in our own backyard – see 'The Pedlar of Swaffham' in Chapter 3. I would often ask groups: 'how long do you think the prince searched for her?'. Some people would say six months or five years but all were impressed when I said twenty years.

The seriousness of the act of burning the frog skin escapes no one. Often, when I tell the story for the first time, people will gasp or groan when I come to that part. They know that it is a mistake even without hearing the consequences. We can sympathise with the prince's desire to have a bride like his brothers, but we must never try to destroy the part of someone that we consider unlovely. If we consider the story's psychological implications we can interpret it thus. We all have a part of us that is unlovely or unattractive which Jung refers to as the shadow. The shadow is any part of us that is unacknowledged and hence rejected. We need to love that part in ourselves rather than try and change it. The paradox is that if we are able to do that then everything is transformed because we begin to access its power from within the self rather than externalising it.

In this story the prince loves the princess when she looks like all the other girls and wants to preserve her as this. He rejects the symbol of her difference from his image of what a woman should look like, that is, the frog skin, and so loses her.

A lot of the stories included in this chapter contain themes of enchantment.

The symbol of enchantment is a story's way of conveying a part of ourselves being spellbound, enthralled (original meaning, enslaved), unchanging. Often it is the unconditional love of another that breaks the spell.

The frog princess and the young prince cannot be together at the point where he destroys her frog skin because in his impulsiveness he tries to rush a very delicate process. In therapeutic terms this is described as 'premature closure'.

Premature closure is where a person rushes to a conclusion rather than allowing a process to unfold. This can also happen if the therapist labels or explains the process before the client has experienced it for themselves. Often the premature closure happens because of the client's or therapist's discomfort with the attendant feelings, which can be frustration, anxiety or excitement. However, if premature closure occurs, as we can see in this story, no true satisfaction is experienced and the process has to begin again and often takes even longer.

Using the story in a session

In an enactment of 'The frog princess' in a day centre we were short of men so the two male members of the group worked very hard to play all three brothers and the king. The group were very insistent that the parts be played by men even though, as an experienced group, they had often taken parts of the opposite gender before.

I shall never forget the part where the men fire their arrows and win their brides. The two women playing the banker's daughter and the merchant's daughter played their roles to perfection. They may have been helped by the fact that everyone was cheering and congratulating the 'young men' on their 'catches'. They fluttered their eyelashes and swished their skirts and one asked her suitor, 'so, do you like what you see?'. This was from a woman who I had always thought of as quite shy and retiring.

All of the group became involved in the baking of bread and embroidering of a shirt. They suggested ingredients and baking times, fabrics and different types of stitches.

At the end of the story, when the prince has been searching for twenty years, one woman asked me, 'how old is he now, then?'. I discussed it with the group and we decided he was probably in his late thirties. The woman nodded sagely and said, 'that sounds about right, he's going to know what's what by now and can really appreciate a good woman'.

The Boa and the Mango tree

Once there was an old woman who had two daughters.

One day she was coming home through the forest when she rested for a moment under a mango tree that was laden with fruit. The mangoes looked so delicious and the woman was so tired that when she heard a rustling in the branches of the tree she called out, 'whoever you are up there, if you could throw me down one of those ripe juicy mangoes I would give you one of my lovely daughters to marry'.

Hardly had she finished talking than a mango came sailing out of the tree and landed in her lap. The woman chuckled to herself and ate the sweet fruit with relish. When she had finished she said, 'I'm off home now so show yourself. I'd like to see who is going to be my future son-in-law'.

All at once there was a great slithering in the tree and out from the foliage emerged an enormous boa constrictor with coil after coil of shiny green skin. The woman was appalled. 'Why didn't you say who you were?' she said. 'You never asked,' said the boa, 'and yes I would really like to marry one of your daughters just as you promised.'

The old woman returned home disconsolate and explained the situation to her daughters.

The elder daughter shrieked, 'marry a slimy old snake, no fear', but the younger daughter said, 'if that is what you agreed then I will marry the boa'.

The next day the boa arrived for his bride and despite the pleas of the old woman he took her off deep into the forest.

Soon they came to the trunk of an enormous tree and the boa led the girl into the trunk and down a passage into the depths of the earth. From below she could see a strange glow and turning a corner she gasped, for there spread out before her was a wondrous underground city full of spires and covered in jewels. She turned in amazement to the boa and there was a beautiful young man. 'Welcome to my kingdom,' he said, 'I am a serpent king and you are my queen.'

The girl was overjoyed and settled down to her new life with alacrity.

On a visit home her mother and sister listened to her tale with amazement. The sister was very jealous. She wished she had offered to marry the serpent after all.

One day she said to her mother, 'I am going into the forest to find a serpent king for myself. Get the house ready. I'm going to bring a husband home'.

Off she went to the forest and it wasn't long before she spied an enormous boa curled up in the branches of a tree. Using a stick she prised it off the tree into a sack and took it home.

Once home she announced to her mother, 'mother, I'm off to bed with my new husband and I don't want to be disturbed'.

Soon afterwards the old woman heard terrible sounds coming from the bedroom. She heard her daughter call out, 'mother, he's up to my knees', then a little bit later, 'mother, he's up to my waist', then soon after that, 'mother, he's up to my neck' and then the mother heard no more.

When she went into the room in the morning there was no sign of her daughter and no sign of her daughters 'husband'.

Themes in the story

There are numerous similarities in this Chinese story with 'Beauty and the Beast' the most obvious being the role of the parent. In that story the impulsiveness of the father arouses the beast's wrath but it is his daughter who must face the consequences and go and live with the beast. In 'The boa and the mango' it is the mother whose thoughtless promise rebounds on her daughter.

Interestingly the story is almost a cautionary tale about not being taken in by appearances. The elder daughter refuses to marry the boa and regrets it. She then makes the fatal assumption that all snakes are princes! There are two issues here. One is the issue of motive. The younger daughter's motives are very unselfish. She agrees to put herself in what looks like a horrifying position for the sake of her mother and to honour a promise made by her mother. The older sister is unwilling to do either of these things. Only when she thinks she can benefit does she make the fatal assumption that all serpents are kings.

The other issue is one of the importance of learning how to discriminate. This is a skill the elder daughter does not possess and that is a sign of her immaturity. As a child we are spoon fed information as we have not yet the experience to make our own decisions. Hopefully, as we grow we are supported and encouraged to weigh up information that is given with what we know about the world from our own experience. This is the adult beginning to think for themselves. The adult is able to mull over experiences and make choices and decisions based on what he or she knows of reality. This is the ability to discriminate.

There are also many similarities with 'The frog princess', where the 'unlovely' one is a frog. In this the 'unlovely' one is a snake but is it any coincidence that both are slimy, reptilian, thought to be wet creatures? Is the story deliberately choosing animals that we would have the most aversion to marrying?

Although the frog princess is enchanted we are not given that impression of the snake king. It seems as if it is part of his nature to be able to appear both in human and reptilian form. He is not enthralled or under some kind of spell. It is reminiscent of an Iroquois story where the girl is very proud and refuses all the men in her tribe and longs for an exciting suitor. She ends up marrying a serpent king and has many adventures, some of which are very frightening. Very often a group interpreted this story as having the moral of 'it's better to marry the boy next door and not yearn for any better'. However, if she hadn't risked she would not have had all those amazing experiences and grown so much as a result.

'The boa and the mango' clearly sees the marriage as positive in the transformation of the boa and the presence of his underground kingdom.

This is a common motif and appears in many Japanese stories as a kingdom existing independently under the ocean. It is like a mirror image of our world – a fantastical world with its own laws and treasures.

Stories often present the greatest riches as coming from underground and this can often symbolise the richness of the unconscious waiting to be accessed.

The good heartedness of the younger daughter is rewarded – she thinks she is marrying a snake but he turns out also to be a prince. Here I think this story is describing a greater psychological maturity than the stories that present the beloved as under an enchantment and have the message 'this person is really a princess, not a frog'. It is a very common situation where someone is in a relationship where they deny or refuse to see sides of the person they do not like. The person is either all good (when things are going well) or all bad (when there is conflict).

Kleinians would refer this back to our first intimate relationship, which is with our mother. The infant is unable to tolerate the reality which is that the person on whom they are most dependent (usually mother) has good and bad aspects. Good, for the infant, means being present and taking care of its every need and bad means not being there when it wants her or not sensing and responding to its need. Instead the infant splits the mother into 'good' mother and 'bad' mother, as if they were two separate people.

As we know, personality development is not dependent on chronological age. Many adults have unresolved issues from infancy that they take into their intimate relationships. A true intimacy depends on being able to acknowledge the parts of the person that we don't like in the person we love. This is a stage in romantic love where some people get stuck. When you first meet someone and fall in love you often only see what you like about the person. With time you begin to recognise aspects of the person with which you are not so enamoured. Some people split the person into two people at this point and say, 'He is not the man I married' and reject the person and move on to someone else. Others are able to accept the whole person and see that their prince can also be a snake, their princess can also be a frog!

Using the story in a session

I used this story with an elderly group of people with dementia.

The objects I brought in included a very ripe mango with a smooth green and red skin and a wonderful smell. Everyone identified it as a fruit and, after much thought, Michael remembered its name. He told us he had been in

Malaysia during the war and they had eaten them then. After the session we cut up the fruit and everyone tried a piece. Not everyone liked the sweet, unusual taste but some people really liked it. However, for most people apart from Michael it was a new experience and a welcome addition to the slightly bland and repetitive nature of the daily diet in the hospital.

Sometimes work with the elderly can focus almost exclusively on reminding people of familiar experiences and forget how refreshing it is to come across something new. It is a myth that a natural consequence of ageing is that people lose curiosity in new things.

I also brought a beautiful wooden snake that was painted bright colours and had niches carved in its length so that, held by the tail, it undulated about in a very snake-like manner.

I was very careful how I introduced this object because of an experience I had on another occasion when I said we were doing a story with a snake in it. A lady looked very alarmed and asked nervously, 'you're not bringing one in here are you?'. Most of the time, if a group is established and there is trust and familiarity, people have a confidence that you are not going to expose them to a frightening experience 'in reality'. Then you can use stories that have scary elements and people really enjoy them knowing 'it is just in the story'.

Michael agreed to play the snake that was also a king and Molly said she would play the younger daughter. I asked my co-therapist to play the elder daughter and Marie said she would play the mother if 'she could just sit here'.

There was a wonderful moment when the serpent king shows his bride his kingdom. Michael drew back his arm and extended it to the group and said, 'see, what do you think of this beautiful place?'.

Everyone had their faces lifted towards him and for a moment we were all included in this image of this magical place.

Alison, my co-therapist, made the most of her role as the elder daughter. She took the wooden snake around the group telling people, 'I'm going to marry him. I think he's a prince in disguise'. Some people really chuckled and Jeanne touched Alison's arm and said, 'now, do be careful, dear'.

We finished the group by thanking everyone for their part in the story and eating the mango.

Epilogue

And so we come to anther ending – the ending of a book.

As we have seen, endings and how we deal with them are very important. We have looked at how many of the elderly people we work with are in a stage replete with endings, and one of our tasks is to acknowledge that fact and give space and opportunity for the range of thoughts and feelings endings can produce in our clients and ourselves.

We have explored the different ways we have of acknowledging endings, with a story, an object, a movement or a song.

We have seen how important it is to acknowledge the ending of each session or activity in the use of a stabiliser or closure exercise.

We have explored our own attitudes towards endings and our feelings around loss. I am not someone who likes endings and my tendency in the past was to try and avoid them. It is only recently, in the last year or so, that I have realised how in doing so I have cheated myself out of a sense of completion and hence satisfaction. More and more I opt to experience the ending fully with all its attendant feelings of loss and regret in order to feel more substantial. However, I am aware as I write that I finished the rest of this book six weeks ago and delivered it to the publisher over a month ago. I have avoided this particular ending until the point when I realised that was what I was doing.

Ending the book means letting go of a process that began three years ago in a conversation with my co-therapist and friend, Alison Kelly. It means letting go of all those wonderful stories so others can share them and all the memories of the remarkable people I have worked with so I can move on. It means recognising that every ending is in fact a beginning and that, in the words of TS Eliot, 'the end is where we start from'.

Index

abilities, maintenance and extension 16, 23-25, 43
  see also expanding horizons
abortion 86
affectionate atmosphere 25
Africa and African stories 13, 56, 65, 81
African drums as objects 65
American stories 13, 45-50, 55, 101
Andersen, Hans Christian 107
apple, wooden as object 158
approach, professional
  emphasis on fun 23
  flexibility in 20, 29
  holistic 15
  person-centred 25
  resistance against 24
Athlone House, Hampstead 10
attention span 28
autonomy loss 89-91

Babylon 96-97
ball, inflatable as object 35, 36
Beauty and the Beast 140, 169
  see also fairy tales
bedside cabinet 122
bereavement 33, 86, 121
Bettleheim, Bruno 52, 133
body language 20, 161-162
bongos as objects 102
boredom 15, 23
boxes as objects 132
brain tumor 134
bridge to storytelling see objects, use of
Buddhist teaching 149
burglary 86, 126
Bury St. Edmunds 107

Caesarian section 75
Campbell, Joseph (mythographer) 75
care in the community 122
casting the story 43-44
catastrophic fantasies 88
chicken toy as object 45
China 13, 61
choice
  of activity 36
  eliciting 26
  encouragement to make 27
  important prerequisite 33
  of involvement level 28
  offering and supporting 25, 34, 43
  and resolving long-past issues 93
Christmas 138
Cinderella 139
  see also fairy stories
closing the story 43
cognitive ability 19
cognitive ability loss 90-91
coma 85
comb, tortoiseshell as object 78
communication
  congruency in 20-21
  emotional tone in 21
  and storytelling 43
community experience 15, 21-22

concentration span 28
confidence building 44
connection
  and communication 20, 21, 43
  lack of, isolation 21, 22
  as social interaction 19
  and the story session 34
  without contact 19, 20
contact
  building 15
  and communication 43
  by conflict 135
  encouragement to make 27
  and group make-up 33
  in intimate relationship 134
  a one-to-one interaction 16, 18
  opportunities for
    fewer when elderly 17
    providing 35
  physical positioning for 19
  and physical touching 18
  power of 44
  quality of 16, 17
  reciprication of 18
  and the story session 34
  verbal incomprehension no bar 19
Cousins, N. 22
creativity 22
crones in fairytales 148
cultural differences 18

Dahl, Roald 133
dancing
  love of 81
  tradition of 102, 152
David and Goliath 163
death
  acknowledgement of 84-85
  attitudes towards 84
  oblique approach to 92
dementia
  and appropriate behaviour 139
  and autonomy, loss of 122, 126
  and behaviour of others 91
  and 'body and soul' analogy 142-143
  and contact 18, 143
  and distinctive personality 143
  and emotional understanding 93
  and inappropriate approaches 24
  and object choice 120, 121
  and person-centred approach 25
  and physical contact 161
  and respecting the individual 28
  and sexual behaviour 137
  and suitable stories 95, 113, 131
Dementia Research Project, Bradford 25
demographics 9
depression 89, 97
depression, and sympathetic contact 97-98
Depression, the 125, 151
dignity, loss of 89, 90
disappointment 86
disregard for elderly see marginalisation of elderly
divorce 86

dreams and stories, similarities 75-76, 136
dreams, symbolic of unconscious 119
Easter 138
ego integrity 84
Egypt and Egyptian mythology 101, 120, 143
Elliot, T.S. 173
emotional indifference 144
endings 92, 173
England 61
English disregard for elderly 64
enjoyment 15, 22, 43
Erickson, Erik 83-84
Europe 13, 148
expanding horizons 11
  see also abilities, maintenance and extension of
fabric, bright as object 10, 37, 38, 48, 66, 132,
faculty retention 24-25
fairy stories 51, 52, 77, 148
  see also Beauty and the Beast, Cinderella, Jack and the Beanstalk, Sleeping Beauty
family and friends 91
fear of growing old 83
feelings, sensitivities 87-88
financial organisation 128
first sessions 10-12
flexibility in approach 20, 29
flirtation 138
format of sessions 92
freedom, loss of 91
Freud, Sigmund 137
Gambia 66
gender roles re-evaluated 136
general practitioner 126
Gilgamesh 85, 101
gown, brocade as object 117
grandparent substitution 86
Greece 121
Greek mythology 96, 101, 107, 112, 162
grief, personal responses 87
Grimm, Jakob and Wilhelm 52, 77
group membership, transition to 35-36
groups
  atmosphere, sensitivity to 33
  encouragement to join 26, 70
  establishment of ground rules 36
  fears of joining 14, 15, 21
  importance of individual within 133
  interaction 10, 12-13
  involvement in 12, 14, 29
  make-up 33
  opportunities for sharing 21
  physical arrangement, shape 34
  stress potential 27
  voluntary participation 34
halva as object 121
Hassidic women 136
Harlow, H.F. 17
hats as objects 37, 71
holistic caring 15
home
  making a house a 113-114

symbolic of self 120
thematic importance 108
homeland 86
Hope and Glory (John Boorman film) 106
human experience, universality 11, 13
identification with roles 93
Ignatieff, Michael 143
imagination as tool 10
independence, loss of 89-91
Indian mythology 145, 162-163
individual, respect for 28-29
infancy, link with old age 17-18
infantilising adults 13
initiative 28, 36, 43
interest buildup 15, 23
involvement levels 12, 29
Irish buran as object 102
Iroquois story 170
isolation 15, 21, 22
    see also marginalisation of elderly
Italy 128

Jack and the Beanstalk 77
    see also fairy stories
Japan and Japanese stories 81, 170-171
Jerusalem 119
jewellery as objects 39
Jews and Jewish tales 107, 119, 125, 134, 136
Johnson, Robert 112-113
Jung, Carl Gustav
    archetypal information 76
    gender archetypes 135
    view on life cycle 83
    mother complex 160
    'shadow' 133, 166
    view on water 113

keep-fit classes 102
Kleinian dichotomy 171
Kubler-Ross, Elizabeth 92, 97

Lamour, Dorothy 66
laughter 22, 25, 35-36, 158
leaves, fallen as objects 99
Lessing, Doris 51
letting go 173
life changes, major 86
limber see warm up
listening 43
London 70, 72, 74, 75, 107, 126, 136, 145
loss
    of belongings 89-90
    of chronological perspective 93
    of health 88
    of home 108
    of memory 91, 123
    of personal security 86
    of pets 123
    of senses 89
    of spouse or partner 91, 101
    of status 90
    of wealth 89-90
loss experiences 86-91, 93, 123
loss, personal responese to 87
loss, self-awareness towards 92

lycra as object 10, 36, 98, 161
Malaysia 171
mango, ripe as object 37, 171
Maori myth 76
marginalisation of elderly 9-10, 51, 64-65
    see also isolation
marriage, fascination of theme 134
Mehrabian, A. 20
microphone toy as object 48-49
Middle Ages 148
miscarriage 86
mother complex 160
motherhood, loss of role 90
mugging 86, 126
myths, existential concerns of 92

nautical theme 132
needles, old in packets as objects 78
negative view of elderly 11, 13
neighbourly trust 126
non-verbal communication 43, 162
    see also verbal incomprehension
normalisation after storytelling 44-45, 49, 50
Northumbrian story 70

objects, mundane received with enthusiasm 10
objects, use of
    affirming individual contributions 38
    attracting attention 39
    as catalysts 10, 12
    and energy levels 37-38
    and enriching experience 36
    guidelines 39-40
    and information provision 38
    limiting number 39
    and opportunities for contact 38
    and respecting individual differences 38
    and retention 40
    and stimulating senses 37-38
    and story introduction 37, 48-49
Oedipus complex 137
old age, link with infancy 17-18
opening the story 43
oral tradition 13
ornament as object 39
Orpheus and Eurydice 96

Paderborn, Westphalia 80
Palestine 106
pantomime analogy 40-41
paralysis 36, 89, 161
Parkes, C. Murray 92
pebbles as objects 120
personal acknowledgement 10
personality development 171
perspective, narrowing of 99
physical contact
    opportunities for 160
    overcoming rejection of 161
playfulness 22, 25
Poland 107
pomegranates as objects 99
positive affirmation 36

post-natal depression 86-87
post-traumatic stress syndrome 106
psychological implications of stories 133

quality of contact 16-17

reading the story 42-43
Red Cross 106
relationship
    building 15
    maintennce 135
ribbon, coloured as object 45
Rogers, Carl 25
role playing 43-44
romantic ideal 134
Romany gypsies 78
Russia and Russian tales 13, 53, 61, 107, 149, 166

St. Pancras hospital 55
saris as objects 145
seaweed as object 132
security, loss of personal 86
self-esteem 15, 17, 22-23
sensitivities, feelings 87-88
separation 86
separation of group see normalisation after storytelling
Sesame 10
sex, a taboo subject 136-137
sexual behaviour in context 137
sexual connotation in action 158
sharing 43
shells as objects 39, 70, 121, 132
shirt, frilly as object 158
shoes, wooden Japanese as objects 81
Sleeping Beauty 107
    see also fairy tales
slippers, brocade as objects 81
snake, wooden as object 172
soap operas 92
social interaction, diminishing availability of 21
social standing, loss of 90
sound effects 71
spatial awareness 98
speaking when storytelling see reading the story
Speech and Drama, Central School of 10
sponge as object 39
spontaneity 22, 26
spouse, loss of 91, 101
stabiliser see normalisation after storytelling
stays, whalebone as objects 78
stealing 126
stereotypes of elderly 51-53
stimulation 23, 32, 44
stones as objects 120
stories
    benefits of action elements 117
    casting 43-44
    opening 43
    personification of negative traits 133
    power of 13
    reading 42
    terminating 43
stories and dreams, similarities 75-76

story sessions
  format 33-34
  interruptions 31
  location selection 30
  practical considerations 30
  sympathetic help 32-33
  room temperature and comfort 30
storytelling
  aims 40
  devices to enhance 43
  emotional connectedness 41
  example in practice 49-50
  flexible progression 41
  and gentle disconnection 45
  by heart 42
  and role playing 44, 48
strawberry, fresh as object 39
stroke 56, 61, 65, 83, 89, 93, 122, 158, 161
Suomi, S.J. 17
Swaziland 13
sweets as objects 81
symbolism 93

tea-time, significance of 122
termination see normalisation after storytelling
testing 24-25
Thatcher, Margaret 32
themes of stories
  acceptance 53-57, 140
  accessibility 72-78
  accessing the unconscious 168-172
  acting on instinct 72-78
  adapting to old age 103-107
  adventure 72-78
  affirmation within ourselves 72-78
  affirming behaviour 126-128
  anger 103-107
  appearances misleading 140, 168-172
  avoidance (of unsuitable partner) 123-126
  change in family circumstances 93-100
  coming together 45-50
  commonplace containing value 153-158
  concentration against distraction 109-113
  conflict resolution 62-63
  co-operation 78-82
  courtship 150-153
  creating from small beginnings 45-50
  death of spouse 140-145
  denial of reality 100-103
  depression, progress of 93-100
  discrimination, learning about 168-172
  disorientation 67-72, 118-123
  elevation from humble origins 150-153
  enchantment 163-168
  endurance 153-158

energy conservation 109-113
escape 67-72
exile 118-123
faith 118-123
fear of being lost 67-72
finding after loss 129-133
flexibility 109-113
friendship 45-50
fulfilment 45-50
good-heartedness rewarded 168-172
grief, misguided attitude towards 100-103
group experience, positive 45-50
growing up 93-100
healing power (of love) 103-107
heroism, improbable 78-82
holding and being held 158-163
hopefulness 45-50
identity assumed 93-100
imagery of elderly, positive 114-117
imprisonment 109-113
impulsiveness 163-168, 168-172
independence, maintenance of 53-57
inner beauty 57-61
innocence, loss of 93-100
internal transformation 146-149
intuitive understanding 72-78
invisibility 78-82
isolation 53-57, 63-67
journeying in arduous conditions 45-50
journeying in hope 72-78
kinship 45-50
learning by doing 103-107
living harmoniously within rules 63-67
loathsome power 146-149
losing and finding 129-133
love 103-107
love transcending status 140-145
love unconditional 163-168
money worries removed 150-153
overcoming obstacles 45-50, 72-78, 158-163
parental over-attachment 158-163
personal autonomy
  realised 118-123
  sought 93-100
positive regard 140
poverty 126-128
power sharing 45-50
premature closure 163-168
projecting our fantasies 153-158
reacting to loss 100-103
realisation of potential 118-123
reassurance 93-100
receptiveness 146-149
recognition and reward 57-61, 150-153
rejection 53-57

relationships
  mother and daughter 93-100
  young and old, mutually satisfying 53-57
repulsive powerfulness 146-149
resourcefulness 129-133
retribution denied 67-72
revival 109-113
rigidity 109-113
safeguarding wealth 123-126
satisfaction at success 93-100
searching for home 118-123
seasonal change 93-100
secrecy 126-128
selflessness 57-61
sensibility and insensibility 153-158
sharing (or not) 126-128
sharing responsibilities 150-153
sight and blindness to recognition 153-158
single-mindedness 109-113, 140-145
spellbound love 158-163
steadfastness 114-117
struggling
  to achieve maturity 93-100
  to achieve togetherness 114-117
  to meet a challenge 72-78
success against odds 78-82
supportive behaviour 126-128
thoughtlessness 168-172
trust, loss of 123-126
understanding, intuitive 72-78
violent abduction 93-100
vision 118-123
vulnerability despite wealth 123-126
wisdom, gaining 129-133
Tibetan mythology 75, 149
trust, building 27, 39, 107
Turkey 81

underload stress 23
underworld scenes 96-97, 145
United States 9

Valentine's day 138
Vaseline 89
Venice 132
verbal comprehension 93
verbal incomprehension 19, 21, 36
  see also non-verbal communication
Victorian psychiatric hospitals 108
Virgin Mary 148
vulnerability of elderly 131

Wall Street Crash 125
warm-up 35-36, 47-49
wedding scenario 138-139
Welsh mythology 113
West of England, the University of the 86
wholeness and sexual archetypes 135-136
World Wars 105-106, 133

Yugoslavian tale 52